EUGENE O'NEILL

and the Tragic Tension

EUGENE O'NEILL

AND THE TRAGIC TENSION

an interpretive study of the plays

DORIS V. FALK

RUTGERS UNIVERSITY PRESS

NEW BRUNSWICK, NEW JERSEY, 1958

For permission to quote, from Arthur Hobson Quinn, A *History of the American Drama from the Civil War to the Present Day*, II (1945), a letter from Eugene O'Neill to Dr. Quinn, we are indebted to Carlotta Monterey O'Neill. Thanks are due also to Carlotta Monterey O'Neill, and to the Eugene O'Neill Collection in the Yale University Library, for permission to use passages from manuscripts in the O'Neill Collection.

Permission to quote from Mary B. Mullett, "The Extraordinary Story of Eugene O'Neill," has been granted by *The American Magazine*, in which the article appeared in November, 1922. The quotation from a letter from Eugene O'Neill to George Jean Nathan, which appeared in an article by Mr. Nathan in *The American Mercury* of January, 1929, is reprinted with permission of *The American Mercury Magazine*, Copyright January 1929. For permission to quote from the Prefaces to the O'Neill plays in the Wilderness Edition of *The Plays of Eugene O'Neill*, III and V, published in 1934, we are indebted to Charles Scribner's Sons. The Citadel Press has given permission to quote from *The Lost Plays of Eugene O'Neill*, published by The Citadel Press in 1958. Material from *Eugene O'Neill: The Man and His Plays*, by Barrett H. Clark (1948) is reprinted through permission by Dover Publications Inc., New York 10, New York. Thanks are due to Harper & Brothers for permission to quote from Francis Fergusson, "Eugene O'Neill," in Morton D. Zabel, ed., *Literary Opinion in America* (1937). Permission to quote from Archibald MacLeish, "You, Andrew Marvell," has been granted by Houghton Mifflin Company. J. B. Lippincott Company has granted permission to quote from Eugene O'Neill, "Memoranda on Masks," which appeared in the *American Spectator Yearbook* in 1934. Thanks are due to the *New York Post* for the use of Mr. O'Neill's letter of February 13, 1926, Copyright 1926 N.Y. Evening Post, Inc. W. W. Norton & Company has granted permission to quote from Karen Horney, *Neurosis and Human Growth* (1950). The quotation from Sam E. Davidson's translation of Strindberg's *To Damascus*, in *Poet Lore*, XLII (1934) appears by permission of *Poet Lore*. Substantial quotations from O'Neill's *Plays* (1954) and *Moon for the Misbegotten* (1952) are made possible through the kind permission of Random House, Inc. Permission to quote from Erich Fromm, *Man for Himself* (1947) has been granted by Rinehart & Company. Simon and Schuster has granted permission to use material from Isaac Goldberg, *The Theatre of George Jean Nathan* (1926). Thanks are due to the Yale University Press for the quotations from O'Neill's *Long Day's Journey Into Night* (1956) and *Touch of the Poet* (1957).

TO MY MOTHER AND FATHER

ACKNOWLEDGMENTS

This book presents an interpretation of the plays of Eugene O'Neill. It is deliberately narrow in scope, confining itself to the tracing of a single, if complex, pattern in the plays and, inevitably, in the mind of the man who wrote them. Some phases of this pattern have, of course, been touched on in varying contexts by many critics, but since the present study is not intended to be a bibliographical compilation of opinions, I have referred only to a few of these in the text.

My chief debt is to the late Professor Henry Alonzo Myers, under whose aegis the idea for this book developed. The finished book is a small tribute to the memory of a keen scholar and a wise man. Students of Professor Myers and readers of his two books, *Are Men Equal?* (1945) and the posthumous *Tragedy: a View of Life* (1956) will recognize his pervasive influence upon my thinking. No listener could fail to respond to Professor Myers' dynamic and perceptive discussions of drama, literature, and philosophy. Among his students he developed not only a following, but a group of independent thinkers and a respectful "loyal opposition" to his views. His death at the age of forty-nine was an irreplaceable loss both to scholarship and to education.

I should like to thank Mrs. Eugene O'Neill for her kind permission to study and quote from the manuscripts in the Eugene O'Neill Collection at Yale. I am grateful to Dr. Donald C. Gallup, Curator of the Collection of American Literature at the Yale University Library for his patient cooperation.

My thanks are due also to the publishers mentioned on the copyright page for their permission to quote from books on their lists.

Finally, I wish to thank the many friends who listened to me patiently or helped with such chores as proofreading and typing. They know who they are and that I am grateful—not least to those who argued and criticized, and to those who refused to take me seriously and offered diversion rather than advice.

DORIS V. FALK
New Brunswick,
New Jersey

CONTENTS

ACKNOWLEDGMENTS vii

THEME 3

QUESTION 14

THE SEARCHERS 25

THE EXTREMISTS 61

THE FINDERS 79

THE TRAPPED 121

THE WAY OUT 144

FATAL BALANCE 156

LONG DAY'S JOURNEY 179

NOTES 202

INDEX 207

There is no steady unretracing progress in this life; we do not advance through fixed gradations, and at the last one pause: —through infancy's unconscious spell, boyhood's thoughtless faith, adolescence' doubt (the common doom), then scepticism, then disbelief, resting at last in manhood's pondering repose of If. But once gone through, we trace the round again; and are infants, boys, and men, and Ifs eternally. Where lies the final harbor, whence we unmoor no more? In what rapt ether sails the world, of which the weariest will never weary? Where is the foundling's father hidden? Our souls are like those orphans whose unwedded mothers die in bearing them: the secret of our paternity lies in their grave, and we must there to learn it.

—Melville, *Moby Dick*

EUGENE O'NEILL

and the Tragic Tension

T H E M E

Eugene O'Neill is the dramatist of an idea. Shouted, whispered, or silently assumed, one theme unites all his plays, from the earliest experiments to his last mature work. The theme is rooted in O'Neill's own personal need, and its power to shape both form and meaning in the plays is derived from this source. It represents an attempt at once to express and to assuage the lifelong torment of a mind in conflict.

O'Neill thought of himself as a writer of "ironic tragedy," but irony requires a detachment which he found impossible. Pity, indignation, despair at the human position, robbed his tragedies of the irony he intended them to convey. The sneer became only the protective mask of a face distorted by suffering; the ironic words were drowned in cries of anguish. The plays are attempts to explain human suffering and, somehow, to justify it. The result is not irony, but the classic twofold justification of the ways of God—or fate—to man: first, that suffering and the very need to explain and symbolize it are the fountainhead of human action and creativity; and second, that fated though he may be, man is ultimately a free and responsible agent who brings most of his grief upon himself through pride.

While this philosophy presents an orderly view of the human situation, it does not imply a sanguine one. If pain and action are inseparable, then it follows that the active, creative, sensitive man is doomed to suffer. He is the one who knows that the desire to express or to avoid grief is the impelling force of life—that pain is the Janus-face of joy; but then he becomes aware of the duality of *all* value. He sees that life and action exist in a perpetual tension between opposites, each of which owes its existence to the presence of the other. This tension is the source of all change and growth, for as night exists only in contrast to day, so night flows eternally into day and day to night again. The life of the race is perpetuated in the flow of natural process from birth to death to birth again; the life of the individual man moves from joy to pain to joy eternally.

The justification of the Fall through Pride also implies a pull between opposites, for here, too, man moves between relative values. The very pride which is the source of his aspiration, enabling him to transcend many of his limitations, can be his destruction when it ignores those limitations and covets godhead. Similarly, the humility which can lead to the *via media* and self-acceptance may take the sick, distorted form of paralysis and self-destruction. Man, according to O'Neill, must find his way somewhere between pride and humility. In his pride he sees himself as exalted conqueror; in his humility, as lowly, self-denying penitent. Each self-conception depends upon its opposite for existence and definition. Just as an active, creative (and necessarily painful) life moves from one value to another, so it must also move from one self-image to another.

This view of life has, of course, a long, familiar history in philosophy and art. O'Neill's conception of process as the unity in which opposites are reconciled has numberless philosophical parallels and sources—in the works of Heraclitus, Plato, Aristotle, Lao-tse, Nietzsche, Emerson, to suggest only a few. The greatest heroes and heroines of O'Neill's plays belong to the literary tradition of the Fall through Pride—the tradition of Prometheus, Oedipus, Tamburlaine, Macbeth, Satan—and Adam, Faust, Ahab. From its very origin in ritual, the drama has always drawn together the elements of process and pride; the same god who was slain and reborn in the primitive rite representing the cycle of seasons is destroyed in later tragedy by his arrogance—*hubris*.

But O'Neill was after all not a Greek, nor an Elizabethan, nor a nineteenth-century Romantic. As a twentieth-century man, he had to interpret the ancient idea in twentieth-century terms and symbols. He found those in the conditions of modern living and in the language of psychoanalysis. O'Neill knew, of course, the general out-

lines of Freudian theory, but his imagination was stimu-
lated most by the work of Jung, and especially by those
Jungian concepts formulated by analogy to the universal
human problems expressed in art, literature, and philosophy.

Jung sees man's primary need not in the desire to satisfy
physical drives or to fulfill any single emotional necessity
such as power, security, or love, but in a longing for a life
of meaning and purpose—for a sense of order in the universe to which man can belong and in which he can trust.
Jung is a mystic in the same sense that O'Neill is mystical:
He recognizes what he calls "psychological truth" as existing independently of objectively provable fact. The constant, eternal longing of the human mind for a universal
order and the expression of the longing in archetypal
symbols constitute what Jung accepts as the "psychological" truth of the existence of such an order. To O'Neill
also, the order of existence which he refers to as "Fate,"
"Mystery," "the biological past" is to be sought in the
forces at work in the human psyche. O'Neill assumes,
with Jung, that one's problems and actions spring not only
from his personal unconscious mind, but from a "collective
unconscious" shared by the race as a whole, manifesting
itself in archetypal symbols and patterns latent in the
minds of all men.

O'Neill uses many of the terms and ideas of the Jungian
system, but most important is this conception of the unconscious as an autonomous force, existing independently
of the individual man but expressed through him. All his
life man is forced to wrestle with the unconscious in an
attempt to reconcile its demands with those of his conscious ego. The Sin of Pride means to O'Neill what it does

to Jung: Man is in fatal error when he assumes that his conscious ego can fulfill all his needs without acknowledgment of the power of the unconscious, the modern equivalent of the gods. Clinically speaking, the ignorance or suppression of unconscious needs results in neuroses and psychoses; poetically speaking, to consider oneself the sole arbiter of one's destiny is to court destruction. On the other hand, the conscious ego must attempt to assert itself, for complete submission to the unconscious drives means withdrawal from reality and action, just as does the fatalistic and complete submission to the "will of God." O'Neill's answer, like Jung's, is the classic one. Men must find self-knowledge and a middle way which reconciles the unconscious needs with those of the conscious ego. This means that life inevitably involves conflict and tension, but that the significance of this pain is the growth which Jung calls "individuation"—the gradual realization of the inner, complete personality through constant change, struggle, and process. *

If O'Neill has consciously echoed some of the thought of Jung, he has unconsciously anticipated the findings of the "Neo-Freudians," Karen Horney and Erich Fromm. They, too, have turned to the humanities for insights to be applied in the clinic. Freud saw man as the victim of animal drives which, at best, could be sublimated to constructive ends. Although the Neo-Freudians revere and use Freud's insights and techniques, they see man as a free and dignified being capable of creating his own destiny. The first, however, of his Deadly Sins against him-

---

* For Jung's statement of his position on the tension between opposites, see especially *Two Essays on Analytical Psychology* in *The Collected Works of C. G. Jung*, VII (New York, 1953), pp. 52–53.

self and others is Pride. This is not, of course, that healthy self-respecting pride which gives men confidence to act; it is instead the false pride that Nietzsche calls "vanity"— the attempt to create oneself according to an impossible, untrue self-image. The sick and swollen ego cannot differentiate between humility and humiliation, and therefore cannot face the reality of its falseness without complete destruction. The victim of this neurotic pride, like the classic tragic hero, has unconsciously rejected his humanity—his real, imperfect self—for aspiration to Godlike perfection. His desperate, unconscious urge to achieve this divinity may drive him forward with the compulsive monomania of a Napoleon or a Hitler; the shame of his inevitable failure to achieve it may cause him willfully to punish or destroy himself, or to seek asylum from the struggle in apathy or death.

The work of the Neo-Freudians, whether or not theirs is the most effective school of modern psychology, both reflects and illuminates the patterns of human behavior which O'Neill described from his own observation and experience. These same patterns are described with varying terminologies in all the major psychoanalytic systems, especially in those of Jung and Adler. The Neo-Freudians, however, particularly Horney, have provided a theory which gives order and coherence to O'Neill's unconscious self-revelations and clearly relates them to his conscious philosophy. To show this correlation, rather than to attempt to determine the ultimate origin of O'Neill's problems in his experience or to wring the last drop of possible subconscious significance from every suggestion of it in the plays, is the purpose of this book. O'Neill's explicit use of psychoanalytic symbols should be warning enough that superficial Freudian guesswork on the part of a lay critic is likely to be off the track of significant truth. One professional analyst, however, Dr. Philip Weissman, in a fascinating article entitled "Eugene O'Neill's Autobiographical Dramas," (*Journal of the American Psychoanalytic Association*, V [July, 1957] pp. 432–460), has interpreted O'Neill's work as sublimation of his own Oedipal drives. According to Dr. Weissman, O'Neill's enforced inactivity as a result of tuberculosis prevented him —and protected him—from acting out in life his unconscious reactions to these drives, and impelled him to express them in his plays. For the literary critic or general reader, however, it is well to remember that the Oedipus complex is as patent a device for plot motivation in O'Neill's plays as the Delphic oracle in Greek tragedy, and has much the same significance; it is one manifestation of the ways of destiny, and becomes, philosophically, a symbol of that destiny. In the light of Neo-Freudian psychology we cannot be misled into thinking that either the parent complexes or the theme of life-sickness (with its solution in what Edwin Engel calls "dream, drunkenness, death" [1]) are mere *substitutes* for philosophy. On the contrary, they are inevitable, orderly steps in its development. The corresponding neurotic pattern does not cancel out the philosophical simply because it elucidates and accounts for it.

O'Neill was impelled by his own deep-seated needs to justify pain, and these needs were the greatest threat to the philosophy which grew out of them. Indeed, within O'Neill's very thesis lurked its antithesis. While he affirmed disintegration as the price of life and pain as the penalty for creativity, there was always the terrible possibility that life and art might not be worth the struggle. Perhaps the price was too high. Perhaps the constant need to establish reality in a world of relative values, to determine one's true identity amid opposite self-images, are sources of a torment as stultifying as it is creative. O'Neill's plays are a consistent chronological record of this torment, charting as clearly, perhaps, as historical biography the direction of his growth as man and artist.

The primary purpose here, however, is less to make the plays reveal their author than to use the author's thought patterns to illuminate his work. Since all of O'Neill's work circles around a basic problem, a given play must be placed in the context of that problem for full interpretation. The problem itself postulates a changing picture of the human dilemma; O'Neill's various descriptions of it and solutions to it proceed in a consecutive chronological order, and it is in this order that the plays should be studied. Obviously, the important dates must be those of the conception and composition of the plays rather than of publication or performance. (O'Neill has provided these for the plays through *Days Without End* in a chronology, with notes, furnished to Richard Dana Skinner for his study, *Eugene O'Neill, A Poet's Quest,* New York, 1935.) Although *The Hairy Ape,* for example, was completed as a play in 1921, it was actually composed—as a short story— in 1917. Since O'Neill rewrote it in dramatic form in only three weeks, the short-story version must have been almost complete as an outline of the play's theme and action. Moreover, *The Hairy Ape* represents an earlier phase of O'Neill's thought; it is logically related to the plays of 1917 rather than to those of 1921.

This very fact that O'Neill's plays are strung like beads

along the all-but-visible cord of an abstract concept not only clarifies their meaning, but also suggests the significant criteria by which they may be measured as drama. The complexities of the idea itself and its relationship to O'Neill's psychological difficulties are the sources of his unique qualities—both virtues and defects—as an artist. Such generally conceded judgments as that O'Neill is skilled in technical theatrics but inept in diction are certainly relevant to an evaluation of his work. The chief concern, however, of a critic of O'Neill must be with the relationship between the play and the consciously formulated idea which underlies it. On one hand, this suggests problems in symbolization, pitfalls of didacticism and allegory. On the other, this relationship between play and basic idea may indicate an additional dimension of meaning, increasing the power of a given play to move and hold an audience.

The nature of the idea itself poses other critical questions. O'Neill is chiefly concerned with the resolution of inner conflicts; with the search for a philosophy which can give order and meaning to such inevitable conflict. What problems in the achievement of dramatic effect are posed by this inwardness of the action? How is the audience to be made to feel the significance of such a private struggle? Each spectator must maintain a double system of values: his own as he watches the character on the stage and that of the character as *he* views the situation. While this is true to a degree in the appreciation of all fiction or drama, it becomes in O'Neill's work a difficulty intensified by the fact that the chief conflict, the real action in the plays, takes place within the mind of the protagonist. And what is the influence of this inwardness on the pace of the drama? Under what conditions can the action move far and swiftly enough to hold audience interest?

Alps on alps arise when the conflict not only is abstract and inward, but happens to be also the author's own personal problem. The very involvement which may give the struggle compassionate authenticity may also prevent the author from creating an objective, directly communicating work of art, may make it difficult for him to free his heroes from himself. At the core of O'Neill's work is his conception of the inward, uniquely personal experience of modern man. Upon the playwright, then, rests the burden of convincing his audience that his heroes, himself, and they are one.

The catalyst compounding art and idea in O'Neill's work is the author's psychological state. It links the dramatic qualities of each play to the central thesis. Pace, tenseness, and reality of action, types and degrees of characterization, repeated but changing symbols, all reveal a state of mind—conscious and unconscious—as much as they do an explicit philosophy. This book does not attempt to create a biography of O'Neill from his plays, nor does it presume to psychoanalyze him, but it does trace an important psychological pattern in the plays which seems to reflect a pattern in the author's psyche.

I have left unexplored some interesting but tangential considerations, largely covered in other sources. I do not try to place O'Neill in the history of the theater, nor do I attempt to establish all the sources (theatrical, biographical, literary) of the plays, but only to suggest enlightening relationships between O'Neill's acknowledged influences and his dominant idea. In the following chapters somewhat detailed descriptions of the plays are included. They are not intended to be plot summaries; they demonstrate and chart the course of the unity between drama and theme. The essence of that unity is the concept of the tragic tension, and the separate plays contain the secret of its unfolding, the beautiful, desperate logic of its progress through the years.

QUESTION

In 1932, when his talent had matured and his reputation was at its peak, O'Neill pleaded for the rebirth of imaginative theater—"a theatre returned to its highest and sole significant function as a Temple where the religion of a poetical interpretation and symbolical celebration of life is communicated to human beings, starved in spirit by their soul-stifling daily struggle to exist as masks among the masks of the living." [1] Ever since 1913, when he had first conceived his mission as priest of this temple, he had been striving for exegesis of its doctrine. What *is* the symbolism with which men celebrate life? What is the nature of the "struggle to exist as masks among the masks of the living"? His early, inept experiments formulated the question and proposed an answer; with refinements, variation, and logical sequences, his later work reiterated it. Not until the last plays, *The Iceman Cometh*, *A Moon for the Misbegotten*, and *Long Day's Journey Into Night*, did O'Neill reveal—to himself and to his audience—the anguished need which compelled him to ask the question in the first place.

Yet, clearly, he asked the question in three of his earliest plays, *Servitude* (*circa* 1914), *Bound East for Cardiff* (also 1914), and *Ile* (1917). *Servitude*, O'Neill's first full-length play, is a clumsy imitation of Ibsen and Strindberg, probably inspired by *A Doll's House* and *Married*, a volume of Strindberg's short stories published in 1913. O'Neill was well aware of the play's deficiencies and never expected to publish it or any of the amateurish efforts included in the same unauthorized volume, *The Lost Plays of Eugene O'Neill* (1950, 1958). In spite of its shortcomings as drama, however, *Servitude* is the statement of an important theme to be repeated and developed throughout O'Neill's work, and its characters have sired dramatis personae which were still walking the boards over forty years afterward.

Mrs. Frazer, the heroine, is the intelligent wife of a wealthy businessman. She has idealized—and idolized—a character from a play entitled, ironically, *Sacrifice* and written by one David Roylston (obviously intended to represent Ibsen). Roylston advocated that a woman should seek full independent self-realization in a career, should not allow herself to be bound in "servitude" to her husband. Mrs. Frazer, like the woman in Roylston's play, leaves her husband and gets a job. Disillusioned, however, by the sordidness and drudgery she encounters, and disturbed by the suffering she knows she is causing her husband, she goes to Roylston for advice. Even more, however, she wants to find out whether or not the playwright lives up to the philosophy he advocates. She discovers that, on the contrary, he has allowed his own wife to devote her entire life to him, has taken her devotion for granted, and has tortured her by infidelity. Mrs. Frazer realizes the falseness of the ideal which had become her own and goes back to her husband, but not until she has convinced Roylston of his own villainy and hypocrisy. She is so successful that he determines to devote the rest of his life to sacrifice for his wife and children. O'Neill makes the moral diagrammatically explicit:

MRS. FRAZER: . . . I asked you to guide my future because I thought you were farsighted. I have discovered you are only in-sighted—as pitifully in-sighted as I was.
ROYLSTON: (*Surprised*) In-sighted?
MRS. FRAZER: Yes, you see nothing beyond yourself. You are so preoccupied with the workings of your own brain that your vision of outside things is clouded. You are only a cruel egotist. (Act III, *Lost Plays*, p. 122)

And later:

MRS. FRAZER: You have the whole future before you for retribution.
ROYLSTON: (*Catching at the word eagerly*) Yes, retribution, joyful retribution every day, every hour! Pay off a part of this enormous debt of love which has accumulated against me. Why, life is going to mean more, be finer and happier than I ever dreamed!
MRS. FRAZER: Happiness is servitude.

ROYLSTON: (*Enthusiastically*) Of course it is! Servitude in love,
love in servitude! Logos in Pan, Pan in Logos! That is the
great secret and I never knew! . . . (Act III, *Lost Plays*,
p. 136)

Obviously, Mrs. Frazer is able to recognize Roylston's
egotism only by virtue of her own, but hers more clearly
than his takes the form of a projected image, almost a day-
dream, of herself. She sees herself in the role of an independent career woman; but this ideal image is a result of
pride—of her own egotism in wanting to expand and develop herself without consideration for her husband. As
soon as, through her experience with Roylston, she recognizes the falsity of her ideal, it falls away and she erects a
new one of self-effacing sacrifice. Thus, in losing self she
has gained self. The difficulty, of course, is that all this
happens on too conscious a level. The reader suspects that
for a woman of Mrs. Frazer's energy, servitude is only
half an answer; she is likely to relapse into independence.

Roylston and Mrs. Frazer, however, are not the only
characters in *Servitude* to be bedeviled by egotistical self-
images. Mrs. Frazer's husband, the stockbroker, sees himself complacently as the perfect Successful Businessman—
the epitome of upright acumen. Mrs. Frazer describes him
thus:

MRS. FRAZER: (*Speaking of her husband*) . . . My family ap-
proved of him in every way. I believe they cherished the
same illusion about his business, in a modified form, perhaps,
as I did.

ROYLSTON: Do you not think your husband also had the same
illusions?

MRS. FRAZER: It would be hard to say. In justice to him I must

acknowledge he always seemed to idealize it. He never could
see his business in all its hideousness as I came to see it, and
I don't think he wore a mask just for my benefit; but you
never can tell. (Act I, *Lost Plays*, p. 80)

The implications of Frazer's illusions about himself and
of his mask vibrate through the entire sequence of O'Neill's
work. In all the plays from first to last, illusion-ridden characters hide from themselves and the world behind a mask.
Always the illusion concerns the character's own identity;
it is a conception of the self. When the character has more
than one self-image, and is not sure which is the true one,
or when he knows that at least one self is an illusion but
still cannot put it aside, he wears a real or figurative mask.

While the theme of *Servitude* may be considered Christian, it is to be noted that nowhere in the play—through
dialogue or specifically symbolic action—is any mention
made of Christ or of religion as dogma. The great discovery of sacrifice is not a revelation from faith but from
human experience. It is a practical formula for self-integration and purposiveness. Not until twenty years later, in
Days Without End, did O'Neill identify sacrifice with
organized Christianity, and then he did so reluctantly.

The characters in *Servitude* are not people, of course;
they are symbols. The transmutation of symbols into living
characters was to be a lifelong problem for O'Neill. He
was always aware that blood cannot flow through the veins
of a character until he has an existence independent of
symbolic meaning, until he springs from the author's mind
and experience fully created and separate from these. The
fascination of a consecutive reading of O'Neill's plays lies
partly in observing the varying degrees of success with

which in his characters he fuses his theories, himself, and a unique individual personality. But the symbolic outlines drawn in his first work persist to the last. The intelligent, gifted male is always Roylston, self-centered, introspective, creative only intellectually; his children are either irrelevant incidents or his enemies. The female is Mrs. Frazer, the eternal mother, the Marguerite who by her love and self-sacrifice redeems the erring male—"Das Ewig-Weibliche zieht uns hinan."

In *Servitude* O'Neill hints at future shadings of the male figure into related types; the playwright and stockbroker in that play become, in later plays, the artist and the businessman, or, less specifically, the introvert and extrovert. In the little one-act play, *Fog* [2] (also 1913–14), this contrast is explicit. The story is slight, and is concerned chiefly with a conflict between two characters, unnamed but labeled "the poet" and "the businessman." The poet is sensitive, idealistic, capable of suffering and sacrifice; the businessman is selfish, narrow, complacent, superficial. With variations, these two are destined to struggle on O'Neill's stage and in his mind throughout his career. They embody the theme of *Beyond the Horizon,* reach full development in *Marco Millions* and *The Great God Brown,* reappear again in *Dynamo* and *Days Without End.* The protagonist is always essentially the poet; the antagonist, the materialist, whether the conflict is between two men, two forces—art and society—or two struggling selves within the same man.

Fog shows O'Neill experimenting with symbolic setting as well as character. The fog in which the action takes place is the same fog of ignorance and fear which surrounds his characters in later plays, even as late as *Long*

Day's Journey into Night. Through this fog sails the S.S. *Glencairn* in *Bound East for Cardiff*,[3] written also in 1914. This was O'Neill's first acted play. Its dramatic vigor has survived, for in it the symbols have blood and bones.

In the chronology of his plays O'Neill included an interesting note on *Bound East for Cardiff*: "Very important from my point of view. In it can be seen, or felt, the germ of the spirit, life-attitude, etc., of all my more important future work. . . ."[4]

As the curtain rises, an injured seaman is dying aboard ship while his comrade sits beside him. The important message is in the attitude of the dying Yank and the reactions of the men around him. Yank accepts his destiny. Life for him has depended for value on an ideal which will never come true, but always remained as a hope, a possibility. Death is to be, in a way, a consolation for the tragedy of the hopelessness of the hope. The tragedy of life makes death less terrible and death makes life seem less tragic. Yank remembers with a sense almost of pleasure his past escapades with his friend, Driscoll—they no longer seem to have been misfortunes, as they did at the time. On the other hand, he hates to go on the death journey alone, for the one positive force of his life has been friendship.

YANK: . . . You mustn't take it so hard, Drisc. I was just thinkin' it ain't as bad as people think—dyin'. I ain't never took much stock in the truck them sky-pilots preach. I ain't never had religion; but I know whatever it is what comes after it can't be no worser'n this. I don't like to leave you, Drisc, but—that's all.

. . . This sailor life ain't much to cry about leavin'—just one ship after another, hard work, small pay, and bum grub . . .

without no one to care whether you're alive or dead. (*With a bitter smile*) There ain't much in all that'd make yuh sorry to lose it, Drisc.

And then the dream of the ideal—which would never have come true—the "pipe dream."

> . . . It must be great to stay on dry land all your life and have a farm with a house of your own with cows and pigs and chickens, 'way in the middle of the land where yuh'd never smell the sea or see a ship. . . . I dunno, this last year has seemed rotten, and I've had a hunch I'd quit—with you, of course—and we'd save our coin, and go to Canada or Argentine or some place and git a farm. . . . I never told yuh this, 'cause I thought you'd laugh at me.
>
> DRISCOLL: Laugh at you, is ut? When I'm havin' the same thoughts myself, toime afther toime. It's a grand idea and we'll be doin' ut sure if you'll stop your crazy notions about —about bein' so sick. (*Plays,* I, pp. 486–487)

Yank's acceptance of death is neither resignation nor simple faith in immortality or God. God, in fact, is a potential enemy, for Yank has killed another man in a fight and fears that God will punish him. Yank accepts the loneliness and the unknown terror with the affirmation of a brave man who has faced suffering before and is prepared to do so again, aware in a dim way that the suffering itself is the source of his ability to bear it. Thus Yank celebrates life in his heroic response to death. He tells Driscoll, "I'm goin' to die, that's what, and the sooner the better! . . . I ain't got a chance but I ain't scared."

After Yank's death the fog in which the ship has been sailing and which Yank felt closing in upon him lifts. This

is his symbolic self-recognition. Bewilderment has given
way before the enlightenment which came with Yank's
awareness and fulfillment of the tragic opposites. Death
not only has been the means of release from life, but has
dignified life by calling forth from the dying sailor his
most heroic qualities—his capacity for friendship and his
courage.

In Yank another archetypal character has emerged. He
is the simple, well-meaning, but blundering natural man.
While not intelligent enough to be either poet or businessman, he has in him the elements of both. He is, in fact,
the poetic spirit—the striving for the infinite—caught in
the restrictions of finite, material reality. In his own way
Yank manages to transcend these limitations by accepting
them as necessary and good. They are the challenge to the
poet in him. Like Ahab in *Moby Dick*,[5] he might have
cried, "Oh now I see my topmost greatness lies in my topmost grief!" But when the character of Yank is developed
to its logical extreme in his namesake in *The Hairy Ape*,
the great wall of finite limitations yields not so easily to
philosophy.

A closer kinsman to Ahab than Yank, however, is Captain Keeney, the monomaniac whaling skipper of *Ile*,
another early one-act play (1917). Here O'Neill plays a
theme in counterpoint to that of *Servitude*. The protagonist is driven to live up to a projected ideal image of himself, but unlike Mrs. Frazer, he never learns to relinquish
it through sacrifice.

Keeney's whaling vessel has been marooned in the
Arctic seas for nearly a year. In addition to his crew, he
has with him his wife, who came on this voyage because
she could not endure the loneliness of waiting for him and

thought that whaling would be romantic, like the voyages of "Vikings in the story-books." Although the crew threatens mutiny, and Mrs. Keeney is going mad with the cold and the monotony, Keeney refuses to return without a full shipment of whale oil. He has a reputation—a self-conception—that he must live up to. He explains that it is not just what the other skippers will think, but *his own self-respect* which is his chief motivation:

MRS. KEENEY: . . . You're afraid the other captains will sneer at you because you didn't come back with a full ship. You want to live up to your silly reputation even if you do have to beat and starve men and drive me mad to do it.

KEENEY: (*his jaw set stubbornly*) It ain't that, Annie. Them skippers would never dare sneer to my face. It ain't so much what anyone'd say—but—(*He hesitates, struggling to express his meaning*) You see—I've always done it—since my first voyage as skipper. I always come back—with a full ship—and—it don't seem right not to—somehow. I been always first whalin' skipper out o' Homeport, and—don't you get my meanin' Annie? (*Plays*, I, p. 547)

Just when Keeney is wavering—almost persuaded by his wife to go home—the ice breaks, the men spot whale, and he determines to go on. His wife does lose her mind, and the play ends with her playing the organ, "wildly and discordantly," while Keeney remains determined to carry on his mad quest for "ile."

Like Roylston and Mrs. Frazer, Keeney pursues a false, egotistical self-image, but unlike them, he never sees the reality. He struggles briefly with this mask of himself, but it is victorious in "stifling" his soul. By sacrificing innocent lives he has sold his soul to the devil in exchange for pride

—a glorified image of his own ego. He has lost his soul in another sense, too, in losing sight of all aspects of himself except that of the successful whaling skipper. This extremism—this monomaniac obliviousness of any values but those of this one mask—is to be the unifying theme of a complete chronological grouping of O'Neill's later works.

Already then, in these seedling plays appear the embryonic outlines of "the symbolical celebration of life" and the "struggle to exist as masks among the masks of the living." The first was hinted at in *Bound East for Cardiff*, where it appears as an affirmative acceptance of life as a conflict of and suspension between opposite values, gaining its very dignity and meaning from this tragic opposition. The very price we pay for living is the experiencing of these opposites, and the only way to reconcile them is to withdraw from life, as the Oriental mystics did in Nirvana but as less extraordinary people may do only in death—the literal death of the body, or the figurative death of the mind and will. O'Neill believed at this time that for living men the true "reconciliation" of the opposites was to live them deeply and endure them courageously.

The struggle to exist as masks among the masks of the living exhibts the same tragic opposition as the life values. *Servitude* and *Ile* show the concern of the protagonists with their own self-conceptions—a concern which in the later plays matures into the Kierkegaardian definition: "The self is a relationship to itself." It is the form and meaning of this relationship and its tragic inevitability which we see emerging from that misty world where wander the "searchers," the protagonists of O'Neill's first group of full-length, finished plays.

THE SEARCHERS

In a letter written in 1925 to Arthur Hobson Quinn, O'Neill stated the objective to which he held consistently all his life:

. . . I'm always, always trying to interpret Life in terms of lives, never just lives in terms of character. I'm always acutely conscious of the Force behind—(Fate, God, our biological past creating our present, whatever one calls it—Mystery certainly) —and of the one eternal tragedy of Man in his glorious, self-destructive struggle to make the Force express him instead of being, as an animal is, an infinitesimal incident in its expression. And my proud conviction is that this is the only subject worth writing about and that it is possible—or can be—to develop a tragic expression in terms of transfigured modern values and symbols in the theatre which may to some degree bring home to members of a modern audience their ennobling identity with the tragic figures on the stage.[1]

In O'Neill's work the "transfigured modern values and symbols" come from psychology. They might have come from economics or sociology or physical science, but the important fact is that they did not. O'Neill specifically and emphatically denies that the political, economic, or physical conditions of modern life are any more than transitory and peripheral. The mystery of fate is an eternal one, not to be mediated or medicated out of existence. It expresses itself significantly not in the external or tangible world, but in the individual human soul. In the manuscript version, only part of which was published, of his author's foreword to *The Great God Brown,* O'Neill says that the theater "should give us what the church no longer gives us —a meaning. In brief, it should return to the spirit of Greek grandeur. And if we have no Gods, [*sic*] or heroes to portray we have the subconscious, the mother of all gods and heroes. . . ."[2] The conflicting social values of today have always existed in one form or another. It is not society which makes us gods or heroes or victims or animals, but the mysterious structure of the mind which must find itself in that society.

To O'Neill God, Fate, Mystery are all aspects of the subconscious and of the struggle of each man to "make the Force express him"—that is, the struggle of the conscious will to assert itself against an unconscious will. This is a tragic struggle, of course, for neither force, the con-

scious or the unconscious, can ever be completely dominant without causing death or insanity. This is not to say
that the conscious-unconscious struggle is the only one
depicted in O'Neill's work, nor that all aspects of mind or
self are represented by these particular opposites. However, even when the conflicting opposites within the self
are apparent to the conscious mind, the very existence of
that opposition is due to some mysterious force exerted by
the unconscious.

And if the principal struggle of man is with his unconscious, self-knowledge must be the first step in his attempt
to control and make constructive use of it. From Socrates to
the psychoanalysts we have understood that the failure
to know oneself results in the tragedy of self-destruction,
in life as in the drama. "For he hath ever but slenderly
known himself," if said of Lear might be said of all those
tragic figures who blunder their way into oblivion, all
those to whom self-recognition comes too late. The conscious effort to overcome this perilous ignorance has been
recorded for centuries in our literature—in the self-questioning of Orestes before the oracle, in the quest of Everyman, in *Hamlet,* in the journey of Conrad's Marlow into
the "heart of darkness." All O'Neill's characters must take
this journey, and at the side of each walks the author.
They set out together in the plays written from 1917 to
1920.

The first of these was *The Hairy Ape,* completed in its
original form as a short story in 1917. Following that came
Beyond the Horizon, outlined in 1917, finished in 1919.
The first draft of *The Straw* was drawn up in 1917, to be
completed in 1919. *Anna Christie,* written and produced
under the title of *Chris Christopherson* in 1919, was re-

vised in 1920 to place greater emphasis on the character of Anna.

The protagonists of all these plays are seeking their proper place in the scheme of things, seeking "to belong"; but their home—the answer to their need—is not to be found in any mystic force outside themselves. It is to be found only in the vast and foggy realms of their own un-conscious, where they seek a self which they can visualize only as a self-image, an abstract identity which will give their lives a direction in which to move.

For these characters one of the chief barriers to under-standing the unconscious is that set up by a conscious ego which perceives its own *limitations* but cannot see beyond them to set up an ideal image. This barrier can be over-come only by death, for the "hairy ape," or by self-sacrifice, for the heroes of *Beyond the Horizon* and *The Straw*. It is not overcome at all by Chris, the old rationalizer of *Anna Christie,* who cannot even perceive that the barrier *is* him-self, but thinks it is "dat ole davil, sea."

The short story from which *The Hairy Ape* developed was drawn from an experience which provided back-ground for at least three of the later plays (*Anna Christie, The Iceman Cometh, A Touch of the Poet*). As a young seaman (1911) O'Neill lived for a period at Jimmy the Priest's, a dilapidated flophouse-saloon on the New York waterfront. In his note to *The Hairy Ape* in the Wilderness Edition he describes the genesis of the play:

It was at Jimmy the Priest's that I knew Driscoll, a Liver-pool Irishman who was a stoker on a transatlantic liner. Shortly afterwards I learned that he had committed suicide by jump-ing overboard in mid-ocean. Why? The search for an explanation of why Driscoll, proud of his animal superiority and in complete harmony with his limited conception of the universe, should kill himself provided the germ of the idea for *The Hairy Ape*.[3]

O'Neill's short story was his attempt to account for the unexplained suicide. He did so by making it the inevitable outcome of a hopeless search for self—the theme of *The Hairy Ape*, unfolding in virtually every line of dialogue and every turn of action.

Yank, the protagonist (namesake of the hero of *Bound East for Cardiff*), begins his story "belonging." He is a stoker on a transatlantic liner. Like the other men, he resembles "those pictures in which the appearance of the Neanderthal man is guessed at. All are hairy-chested, with long arms of tremendous power, and low, receding brows above their small, fierce, resentful eyes." Yank, however, "seems broader, fiercer, more truculent, more powerful, more sure of himself than the rest. They respect his superior strength—the grudging respect of fear. Then, too, he represents to them a self-expression, the very last word in what they are, their most highly developed individual." (Scene I, *Plays*, III, pp. 207–208) Yank sees himself as the others see him—his self-conception is all of theirs and more. Nothing troubles him, no considerations of beauty, of home, of love, of his relation to society—the yearnings of other men expressed in the drunken reminiscences of the old Irishman, Paddy. All that, according to Yank, belongs in the past, is dead; Yank is alive, he is the power behind the ship—behind the modern world:

. . . I'm smoke and express trains and steamers and factory whistles; I'm de ting in gold dat makes it money! And I'm what makes iron into steel! Steel, dat stands for de whole ting! And I'm steel—steel—steel! I'm de muscles in steel, de punch behind it! . . . Slaves, hell! We run de whole woiks. All de rich guys dat tink dey're sump'n, dey ain't nothin'! Dey don't belong. But us guys, we're in de move, we're at de bottom, de whole ting is us! (Scene I, *Plays*, III, p. 216)

Yank neither requires nor respects thought or dreams— "What's tinkin' got to do with it?"

This confident self-image is soon destroyed by Mildred, a pale, repressed young woman whose father is "president of Nazareth Steel, chairman of the board of directors of this line." Mildred is a decadent, aimless, artificial product of society, who dabbles in social work to uplift the masses. When Mildred sees Yank, she falls back in horror, crying "Take me away! Oh, the filthy beast!" and faints. As Paddy says, "Sure, 'twas as if she'd seen a great hairy ape escaped from the Zoo."

For some reason which his primitive intelligence cannot fathom, Yank no longer feels after this incident that he "belongs." He tries dimly to think through the cause of his unrest (after this point he is described repeatedly as assuming the pose of Rodin's *Thinker*). He has been "insulted in some unknown fashion in the very heart of his pride." He can think only of Mildred's image of himself as a brute—an image which takes its form from consciousness not of power, but of limitation. The muscular strength which made him feel superior before, now only identifies him with animals, with the body itself, not with the power that body can produce. Since Mildred has stripped away the ideal which dignified that body and the slow mind within it, the body has become the only symbol of the self,

and constitutes a prison. From this point onward, Yank
devotes himself to an attempt to escape the prison in
which he cannot be content to "belong," but every effort
to escape only makes him more aware of the strength of
the barrier; and the more conscious he becomes of it, the
more hopeless it is for him to attempt to tear it down and
to see himself again as a heroic human being. Ultimately,
he abandons the search as futile and surrenders himself to
the only self-image of which he can be conscious—that
symbolized by the ape and the cage.

Yank sees his first possibility of restoring his old self-
respect in revenge upon Mildred. He looks for her in order
to insult her—"I was goin' to spit in her pale mug, see!"—
but she is heavily guarded, and he cannot reach her.

A shipmate takes him to Fifth Avenue and advises him
to avenge himself on that class of society which Mildred
represents. He tries to do so by assaulting some passers-by,
still asserting, "I'm steel and steam and smoke and de rest
of it!" but finds himself in jail as a result. The development
of the symbol of the steel which, as Yank says, "stands for
de whole ting," charts the progress of Yank's search for
self. In Yank's mind at this point the power represented by
steel no longer appears to be his own, but that of Mildred's
father, which through her has made of steel Yank's prison—
symbolized by the steel bars of the jail in which he is now
actually imprisoned:

Sure—her old man—president of de Steel Trust—makes half de
steel in de world—steel—where I tought I belonged—drivin'
trou—movin'—in dat—to make her—and cage me in for her to
spit on! Christ! . . . He made dis—dis cage! Steel! (Scene VI,
Plays, III, p. 244)

His next step, then, upon release from jail, is vengeance upon the father's steel mills and the social structure they represent. He goes to the office of the I.W.W. to offer his services in bombing the steel mills—an activity which he has been convinced by propaganda is typical of that organization. He is promptly thrown out as a fool or spy, and as he picks himself up, he realizes the final truth, that the source of his trouble is not in society nor in Mildred, but in himself. The very steel which he thought he *was*, is his cage—he himself is his cage, and in the cage sits the conscious ego which looks like a hairy ape.

Dis ting's in your inside, but it ain't in your belly. . . . It's way down—at de bottom. Yuh can't grab it, and yuh can't stop it. It moves, and everything moves. It stops and de whole woild stops. Dat's me now—I don't tick, see? . . . Steel was me and I owned de woild. Now I ain't steel, and de woild owns me. (Scene VII, *Plays*, III, p. 250)

Since he can belong neither to steel—the image of himself as a strong productive power—nor to "de woild"—society, his last resort is to withdraw behind the barrier and surrender to the only self-image with which he thinks he can become integrated, that of the ape. In his final speech and action at the ape's cage all the threads of symbolism are drawn together. Yank sees himself as being between heaven and earth. He cannot belong to the rest of mankind, who have a sense of the spiritual—"I got it aw right . . . on'y I couldn't get *in* it, see? I couldn't belong in dat. It was over my head"—nor can he see himself as a purely animal part of nature. He has no past in which to place himself, no resource in conscious memory or his mind for security. To the ape he says:

Youse can sit and dope dream in de past, green woods, de jungle and de rest of it. Den yuh belong and yuh can laugh at 'em, see? . . . But me, I ain't got no past to think in, nor nothin' that's comin', on'y what's now—and dat don't belong. (Scene VIII, *Plays*, III, p. 253)

Yank pries open the door of the cage and the ape scrambles out. Yank offers the ape his hand with an ironic invitation to join him against the world. But the ape seizes Yank in a crushing hug; then throws his body into the cage and escapes. Caught in the steel cage of self and crushed in the bonds of the ego's self-image, the dying Yank

. . . *grabs hold of the bars of the cage and hauls himself painfully to his feet—looks around him bewilderedly—forces a mocking laugh*) in de cage, huh? (*In the strident tones of a circus barker*) Ladies and gents, step forward and take a slant at de one and only—(*His voice weakening*)—one and original —Hairy Ape from de wilds of—(*he slips in a heap on the floor and dies. The monkeys set up a chattering, whimpering wail. And, perhaps, the Hairy Ape at last belongs*). (Scene VIII, *Plays*, III, p. 254)

When Yank falls to the floor of the cage he is finally integrated with the image of himself as the hairy ape. The long *agon* with the mask is over, and so is life. For life to O'Neill consists largely in this very struggle of the self with itself—a concept suggested in *The Hairy Ape* and destined to reach its full development in the discovery of "the finders." In the form in which it now appears, however, O'Neill is saying that the motion and the spirit that impels all thinking things is the search for identity. In saying so he has extended the symbolism of Yank's struggle beyond psychology to philosophy and, in a sense, to anthropology. The search for identity not only is a personal and individual problem, but becomes the collective, universal problem of mankind. O'Neill explained this meaning in a letter to the *New York Herald Tribune* of November 16, 1924:

The Hairy Ape was propaganda in the sense that it was a symbol of man, who has lost his old harmony with nature, the harmony which he used to have as an animal and has not yet acquired in a spiritual way. Thus, not being able to find it on earth nor in heaven, he's in the middle, trying to make peace, taking the "woist punches from bot' of 'em." This idea was expressed in Yank's speech. The public saw just the stoker, not the symbol, and the symbol makes the play either important or just another play. Yank can't go forward, and so he tries to go back. This is what his shaking hands with the gorilla meant. But he can't go back to "belonging" either. The gorilla kills him. The subject here is the same ancient one that always was and always will be the one subject for drama, and that is man and his struggle with his own fate. The struggle used to be with the gods, but is now with himself, his own past, his attempt to belong.

O'Neill's view of the human dilemma here—and in the later plays—suggests that of Sartrian existentialism. Man's very "lostness," his need to belong, is the key to his humanity. As soon as he has "belonged" he has abdicated his manhood, has ceased to be an "existent" and becomes a passive, vegetative being at the mercy of forces outside himself and beyond his control. Yet all the forces which offer him a secure environment in exchange for obedience and conformity—society, the authority of religion, of the state, of tradition—have been created by man himself. They have no existence of their own except by virtue of man's existence. He is, in actuality therefore, free from all outside authority in the determination of his fate, but he is also the lonely bearer of a terrifying responsibility for himself and the race. He has nothing on which to lean for support but himself, nothing to blame for his failures but himself. Human life has no intrinsic meaning or order —no harmony like that of nature—except the meaning that man projects upon it. He must create his own values and impose upon his universe whatever significance and whatever moral order he expects to adopt as a *raison d'être* or as a basis for an ethical code. To seek asylum from this responsibility for his own destiny by accepting some established institution as an absolute is to escape from the self and from fears of its inadequacy. All man can really hope to belong to is himself. His "sickness unto death" is not his loneliness and anxiety in making choices and bearing responsibility, but what Kierkegaard called "despair at willing to be oneself"—the despair of Yank in *The Hairy Ape*, and of a long line of protagonists in O'Neill's plays.

Obviously, if one takes the view that the source of man's difficulty and the hope of his controlling it lie within the self of each individual man, then the proper study of any humanistic philosophy is the nature of that self. And here the boundaries between the provinces of philosophy and psychology are dim indeed. The findings of psychoanalysts in their efforts to anatomize the self can be considered not only to have individual therapeutic significance, but to illuminate ethical and social problems as well.

Psychoanalysis has had least bearing on ethical principles when it has considered man as a being at the mercy of physical, emotional, and societal forces to which he must adjust. It has had most relevance to ethics when it has considered man as a free and responsible person who must understand himself, and whose self-knowledge is not an automatic cure for his ills, but only a preparation for an active, self-determined life. There is deep significance in the fact that the psychoanalytic theories which are reflected—consciously or unconsciously—by O'Neill's work are those of the psychologists who take this latter position. Erich Fromm, in *Man for Himself*, subtitled, "An Inquiry into the Psychology of Ethics," has stated the dilemma in words which almost paraphrase O'Neill's explanation of *The Hairy Ape:*

> Self-awareness, reason, and imagination have disrupted the "harmony" which characterizes animal existence. Their emergence has made man into an anomaly, into the freak of the universe. He is a part of nature, subject to her physical laws and unable to change them, yet he transcends the rest of nature. He is set apart while being a part; he is homeless, yet chained to the home he shares with all creatures. . . . Being aware of himself, he realizes his powerlessness and the limitations of his existence. . . .
>
> Reason, man's blessing, is also his curse; it forces him to cope everlastingly with the task of solving an insoluble dichotomy. . . . Man is the only animal for whom his own existence is a problem which he has to solve and from which he cannot escape. He cannot go back to the prehuman state of harmony with nature; he must proceed to develop his reason until he becomes the master of nature, and of himself.[4]

To Fromm, as to O'Neill, the tragedy of the need to belong lies in man's desperate drive to identify himself with *one* aspect of his nature, when he is doomed to participate in both; to be both animal and man, flesh and spirit, materialist and idealist. In O'Neill's scheme any or all of these identities can be considered only as the self-image—as a figurative mask or many masks. While in O'Neill's view the struggle to exist among the masks may be soul-destroying, the projection of the masks is life-giving; for it is toward one self-image or another that we move. The self unrelated to itself, that is, without an image toward which to move, cannot progress in any direction. Therefore, according to O'Neill, we must, for life's sake, project a self-image, but it is in the nature of that image that the secret lies. If, like Yank's self-image, it takes its form from the limitations of the self as Yank knows it empirically (*i.e.,* from his conscious ego), it is completely barricaded within itself. The projection must have also an infinite, ideal quality, transcending the conscious ego; it must lead outside the steel cage of itself. This is what Robert, of *Beyond the Horizon,* perceives. But what he makes of it is another matter.

Robert is another searcher for self, as, unconsciously, are his wife, Ruth, and his brother, Andrew. The play is like a fugue, developing with variations the theme of the suspension of life between opposites. We feel the balancing pull not only between reality and idealism, but also between the earthy and the spiritual, joy and sorrow, love and hate, hope and despair. The opposites are symbolized not only in the action of the play, but also in the division of the acts into alternate indoor and outdoor scenes. Of these divisions O'Neill said in a magazine interview:

In *Beyond the Horizon* there are three acts of two scenes each. One scene is out of doors, showing the horizon, suggesting the man's desire and dream. The other is indoors, the horizon gone, suggesting what has come between him and his dream. In that way I tried to get rhythm, the alternation of longing and of loss.[5]

Robert is a poetic dreamer who was a childhood invalid. From his pain grew the longing for beauty which he thinks must lie in the unknown beyond the horizon.

I used to stare out over the fields to the hills, out there— (*He points to the horizon.*) and somehow after a time I'd forget any pain I was in, and start dreaming. (Act I, Sc. i, *Plays*, III, p. 99)

At the opening of the play this romantic longing has ripened into action—Robert is about to leave the farm for a three-year voyage to the beautiful foreign world beyond the horizon. On the eve of departure, however, he discovers that his brother's fiancée, Ruth, actually loves him and not Andrew. Having long been in love with Ruth, Robert remains behind to marry her, feeling that love is perhaps what he had hoped to find in his search. Andrew sails in his place, and Robert hopefully accepts his new position as a family man and farmer.

Shortly after the marriage reality crowds in upon romance, and in a few years the farm has deteriorated under Robert's management and the family are destitute. Supported, however, by the love of his wife and child, Robert clings to his early idealism—only to have another illusion destroyed when he discovers his wife had decided after a month of marriage that she was in love with Andrew. Ruth herself places a foolish hope in something "beyond the horizon" when she expects the returning Andrew still to love her, for he had forgotten Ruth six months after sailing. Now neither she nor Robert sees any meaning in life beyond the love of their child, for whose sake they continue to live together. The ultimate blow comes when the child dies—and their divergent reactions to this loss give the key to their characters.

Ruth is defeated. She withdraws into complete apathy. Robert, now seriously ill with tuberculosis, still reaches out desperately for assurance that happiness may be found somewhere beyond the limits of reality. There must be some self-image to which he can conform besides that of the abject failure; perhaps he would be successful in the city. They can move there to find the secret beyond the horizon. Aglow with optimism, he says to Ruth: "Listen. All our suffering has been a test through which we had to pass to prove ourselves worthy of a finer realization. . . . And now the dream is to come true!" (Act III, Sc. i, *Plays*, III, p. 151) Robert goes to the window to see the sun rise, but reality again denies the dream: "No sun yet. It isn't time. All I can see is the black rim of the damned hills outlined against a creeping grayness."

The black rim of hills can disappear for Robert only when the grayness of death has finally crept over them. At that moment the imprisoning hills of material reality—of the finite limitations of the self—fade before a truer revelation for Robert of the secret beyond the horizon. As in *Bound East for Cardiff*, death provides an enlightenment of life. Robert at last sees clearly the nature of his search and that of Andrew and Ruth. They have all taken their self-images from a false ideal formed by the needs of the ego—when by losing the ego in sacrifice they might have found a new, attainable, and richer ideal. In Robert's dy-

ing speeches O'Neill makes this explicit, as he does the
significance of the tragic suspension between opposites.
The suffering does have meaning, but not because there is
hope of relieving it—the suffering itself frees us from pride.
It gives birth to sacrifice, loss of self, and happiness, just
as Robert's early pain gave birth to his dream of the beauty
beyond the horizon. When Robert comes to accept the inevitable—at the point of death, however, when it is too
late to use his knowledge—this meaning becomes clear to
him and he regains his self-respect; he finds his own ideal,
poetic, "selfless" self that has so long been lost. With conviction he says to Andrew:

Because I'm dying is no reason you should treat me as an im-
becile or a coward. Now that I'm sure what's happening I can
say Kismet to it with all my heart. (Act III, Sc. i, *Plays*, III,
p. 160)

Then he inquires of Andrew, who has lost most of his
money gambling in wheat, what he has been doing in the
intervening years. On finding out he says to his brother:

I've been wondering what the great change was in you. . . .
You—a farmer—to gamble in a wheat pit with scraps of pa-
per. There's a spiritual significance in that picture, Andy. (*He
smiles bitterly.*) I'm a failure, and Ruth's another—but we can
both justly lay some of the blame for our stumbling on God.
But you're the deepest-dyed failure of the three, Andy. You've
spent eight years running away from yourself. Do you see
what I mean? You used to be a creator when you loved the
farm. You and life were in harmonious partnership. And now—
. . . So you'll be punished. You'll have to suffer to win back—
(Act III, Sc. i, *Plays*, III, pp. 161–162)

Robert's last act of sacrifice is to ask Andrew to take care of Ruth. As he dies, on the same hill where the play opened, Robert says:

The doctor told me to go to the far-off places—and I'd be cured. He was right. That was always the cure for me. It's too late for this life—but— . . . You mustn't feel sorry for me, beginning—the start of my voyage! I've won to my trip—the right of release—beyond the horizon!

Ruth has suffered—remember, Andy—only through sacrifice —the secret beyond there—(*He suddenly raises himself with his last remaining strength and points to the horizon where the edge of the sun's disc is rising from the rim of the hills.*) The sun! . . . Remember! (*And falls back and is still. . . .*) (Act III, Sc. ii, *Plays*, III, pp. 167–168)

Robert's idealism has been both his bulwark and his destruction. His spirit, in comparison to Ruth's, is invincible. Death seems to him to bring insight and triumph over all the ills of body and soul. But here, as in later plays, O'Neill is contrasting the inner, subjective view of the protagonist with the outward one. Seen objectively, Robert's death is an escape, not a victory. It is a sorry compensation for a barren life, wasted in a futile search for identity. Robert has never accepted and embraced the tragic opposites which constitute the boundaries—the horizons—of real life. His effort to transcend them is a negation of life, an affirmation only of death. O'Neill rings downs the final curtain, not on the exultant death of Robert, but on Andrew and Ruth, who must remain in the real world. The rhythmic "alternation of longing and of loss" ends on a note of loss. The closing lines of the play turn the audience's attention to Ruth as she listens to Andrew's frantic plea for some sort of new start for them both. (Act III, Sc. ii, *Plays*, III, pp. 168–169):

ANDREW: . . . I—you—we've both made a mess of things! We must try to help each other—and—in time—we'll come to know what's right—(*Desperately.*) And perhaps we—(*But Ruth, if she is aware of his words, gives no sign. She remains silent gazing at him dully with the sad humility of exhaustion, her mind already sinking back into that spent calm beyond the troubling of any hope.*)

(*The Curtain Falls*)

Beyond the Horizon was an exciting and important event in the development of American drama. It was a play with a serious, true, significant message, appearing at a time when the stage was cluttered with trivialities and platitudes. But the very fact that it does illustrate a definite philosophical concept, that that concept is O'Neill's own and must be understood by the audience, and the dual nature of the concept itself, all help account for the neglect of *Beyond the Horizon* at the present time.

Because the message of the play concerns contradictions, its final scene appears to be a contradiction—except, of course, in the specific context of O'Neill's philosophy of opposites. The audience is left with a feeling of having had an emotional experience, but the experience is confused. Robert is the protagonist and has apparently achieved his goal. His death brings with it an implicit resurrection in the form of his exultant insights; but the truth of the resurrection is negated by the final scene. What appeared to be a tragic affirmation of man's nobility in the face of inevitable suffering turns out to be a study in frustration, where weak and foolish people waste their lives. This may be exactly what O'Neill wants us to see, and perhaps we, the audience, are at fault in expecting more. The fact remains that the "alternation of longing and of loss" culminates in a total effect not of rhythm, but of bewildering paradox, to which the final solution seems really to be Ruth's—withdrawal from Nothing into Nothing.

O'Neill's conscious, publicly stated life-attitude was, as he said, the affirmative one of *Bound East for Cardiff*, but the concluding scene of *Beyond the Horizon* suggests a deeper and perhaps more accurate version of his philosophy—one which he found difficult to face. Never again until his last plays was he able to ring down the curtain on a scene as desolate as this one; in the conflict between hope and despair the victor could never be despair. This fact is at the root of some of O'Neill's most serious difficulties in achieving dramatic effect.

As a poetic idealist, Robert is necessarily a mystic, and his mysticism—an inward force—is opposed to the outward logic of facts. Dramatic action, however, must develop logically. It does so up to the point of Robert's acceptance of his imminent death. A major mistake, brought about largely by their own egoism, has thrown three lives out of harmony with existence (as O'Neill would say). Steady disintegration has been the result, and the characters are searching to re-establish harmony. The moment of death is Robert's "epiphany." The insight he suddenly achieves comes not, however, from experience, but from intuition. Robert's inner and outer experience might logically have led him to the acceptance of death as a release after long suffering, but not necessarily to a revelation that sacrifice is the secret of life. Even if his conclusion could be said to have a psychological or poetic logic of its own, Robert's sudden arrival at such a conclusion makes it seem to be a *non sequitur.*

The problem is more complex than simply that of a breach of logic or of a clumsily contrived revelation from the gods or from their mother, the subconscious. O'Neill felt, with Nietzsche, that tragedy is an affirmation—a "symbolical celebration"—of life. The death of the hero must reveal the dignity, nobility, and universality of his struggle, even though from the beginning it has been a futile one. In fact, in this very futility is its magnitude and its implied hope for the rest of mankind. For the hero has willfully or through ignorance violated the inexorable order of the universe or of his own destiny. At his downfall this order is restored. Both the hero and the audience understand the order and know that salvation lies in accepting it.

In the Greek tragedies the order is symbolized in fate or the gods; in Shakespeare it is in the laws of "nature," or of human justice or reason. The hero flouts this order on the stage by his actions; he *dramatizes* his struggle, and when he is destroyed and order is restored both the destruction and the restoration are logical and inevitable. If they are not so but are the result of a fortunate accident or of the intervention of some force not integrated into the play, the drama may have an affirmative ending, but its affirmation will not be that of tragedy. The world is just as meaningless and disordered as ever, even if the hero survives.

In O'Neill's work the violated order is that of the mind; when order is restored, it is restored in the mind. In the Greek and Elizabethan tragedies characters *act* the consequences of defiance, or at least suffer them visibly on the stage. Self-recognition is brought home to them by a progression of events, not by revelation. When, however, the affirmation itself is chiefly in the reorganization of a mental attitude on the part of the protagonist, the playwright is strongly tempted to restore order through revelation, which must be explained in a dying soliloquy or projected through the devices of the expressionistic theater. This temptation to explain or project rather than to dramatize in action may lead to the double weakness of *Beyond the Horizon:* first, that the tragic affirmation lacks convincing logical steps, and second, that it has become explicit. The result is no longer drama, but at best is lyric poetry and at worst, prosaic exposition.

The specter of this problem has loomed before, in *Servitude* and *Bound East for Cardiff;* it was to pursue O'Neill in many of his later plays. In them the shadow of its implication widens to include not only philosophy and dramatic technique, but suggestions of neurosis. That widening begins in the two subsequent plays, *The Straw* and *Anna Christie.*

In *The Straw* (1918) the search for self proceeds in the same direction, amid the same ambiguities, as in *Beyond the Horizon.* The hero finds himself—or thinks he does—at the moment of negation of self. His discovery, like Robert's, is an affirmation of idealism in the face of an insuperably negative reality, but the rhythm of longing and loss now becomes synchronized in a "hopeless hope."

Briefly, *The Straw* is the love story of Eileen Carmody and Stephen Murray, two patients in a tuberculosis sanatorium. Eileen, the daughter of a drunken Irish widower, has come to the sanatorium ill and exhausted from the care of a large family. Stephen has been a reporter on a small town newspaper, who welcomes his stay in the sana-

torium as a rest from the tedium of his job and as a chance
to find some new direction for his life. He has always
wanted to write fiction and at Eileen's suggestion begins
his career as a writer while he is in the hospital. Eileen
falls in love with him, but although Stephen is grateful and
affectionate he cannot return her love.

After a few months Stephen is well enough to leave the
sanatorium. He has no real home to return to, but plans
to visit his two married sisters, although as he tells Eileen,
the sisters "have never seen the real me and never wanted
to." Eileen's answer is,

. . . What is—the real you? (*Murray kicks at the stones impa-
tiently without answering. Eileen hastens to change the subject*) And then you'll go to New York?

Before Stephen leaves for New York, Eileen confesses
her love. In the weeks that follow she grows steadily
worse, having no desire for recovery, until she is beyond
help. Stephen, whose life has resolved itself into aimless
wandering and dissipation, returns to the hospital to visit.
Learning there of Eileen's hopeless condition and his par-
tial responsibility for it, he determines to ask her to marry
him in order to give her at least a short period of happiness.

In the act of proposing, Stephen realizes that he actually
does love Eileen. At the moment of apparent sacrifice he
finds self-realization; his life finally has direction. But
with his awareness of a new life comes also his knowledge
of death and the fear of losing what he has just won. To
Eileen he says (Act III, *Plays*, III, p. 412):

Oh, what a blind selfish ass I've been. . . . I love you, Eileen! I do! I do! And we'll be married—(*Suddenly his face grows frozen with horror as he remembers the doom. For the first time the gray spectre of Death confronts him face to face as a menacing reality.*)

Stephen cannot and does not accept death as the final reality. He tells the nurse who has befriended him and Eileen that somehow his love will conquer death, but the nurse denies his hope by "the pitying negation in her eyes."

STEPHEN: Oh why did you give me a hopeless hope?
MISS GILPIN: Isn't everything we know—just that—when you think of it? (*Her face lighting up with a consoling revelation*) But there must be something back of it—some promise of fulfillment—somehow—somewhere—in the spirit of hope itself. (Act III, *Plays*, III, p. 415)

Clutching at this "straw," Stephen and Eileen plan an impossible future. Again, as in *Beyond the Horizon,* all the logic of events leads to the conclusion that this is a story of waste and loss brought upon a character by his inability to find himself. The message becomes affirmative, however, through revelation, intuition, and explanation. The nurse voices the intuitive "psychological truth" that the endless desire for hope gives validity to the hope itself. Although O'Neill never quite relinquished this idea, he viewed it with growing irony and awareness of the thin line between "psychological truth" and illusion.

The setting of *The Straw* is drawn, of course, from O'Neill's own experience in a sanatorium in 1912–13. Like Stephen, he had come there from a job as a reporter—on the New London, Connecticut, *Telegraph*. Like Stephen, O'Neill discovered his real vocation during this period of enforced rest. There is, however, a hint here of closer identification than this literal one between the author and his hero. For Stephen is still another archetypal "man as artist." He is the supersensitive creative artist, cut off from himself and from others by his own egotism. Born in *Servitude*, he lived O'Neill's lifetime.

Furthermore, although the play begins as the story of the two lovers, the character of Stephen grows out of bounds and runs away with it at last. The dramatic interest is originally in Eileen, but the thematic interest is in Stephen. Most of the action on stage is Eileen's story— her family problems, her love, her slow decline. Yet she is a passive, helpless victim of the absent hero, and even when Stephen returns he does not come back to her, but to himself. The climax of the play is his, not hers; in other words, O'Neill could not decide whose play this was. He was to encounter the same problem in *Anna Christie*, but there he set about solving it consciously and deliberately.

The leading role in the first version of *Anna Christie*, originally entitled *Chris Christopherson*, was that of the father; O'Neill had in fact called the play "a character study of an old Swede." [6] When the first early performances of *Chris* were unsuccessful O'Neill revised the play, emphasizing the character of Anna. In a letter to George Jean Nathan he defined his purpose:

From the middle of the third act I feel the play ought to be dominated by the woman's psychology. And I have a conviction that in dumb people of her sort, unable to voice strong, strange feelings, the emotions can find outlet only through the language and gestures of the heroics in the novels and movies they are familiar with—that is, that in moments of great stress life copies melodrama.[7]

The result, however, is that although "life copies melo-drama" the melodramatic is not necessarily lifelike. Anna's character has a theatrical quality which contributed to the audience's feeling—deplored by O'Neill—that here was an O'Neill play which, for once, had a "happy ending."

Although the action of the play now centers in Anna, the message is still in the character of her father. Chris should have been a searcher for self, but is, instead, a fugitive. Every time he is confronted with his self-image he retreats, and his withdrawal not only forces him to lead an aimless, undirected life, but thwarts and inhibits the lives of the other characters.

Once a sailor, Chris has now retired from the sea and is a barge captain. The sea is to him the devil, the cause of all his hardships and losses. The irresponsibility which has caused him to neglect the wife and children whom he loved came, he thinks, from the influence of the sea—the same sea which made widows of so many of the women of his village. The true sea, however, is himself.

Trying to protect Anna from the influence of the sea (*i.e.*, from marrying a sailor), he boards her with cousins who live inland and thus escapes his own responsibility for her upbringing. The ironic result is that she is seduced by one of the cousins, becomes a prostitute, and sick and dis-couraged comes back to her father—who knows nothing of her true past. On the coal barge with him, Anna feels that she "belongs," is purified and, in a sense, virginal again. She falls in love with a sailor—the very fate Chris had sought to prevent—and Chris opposes the marriage, obviously because Mat, the lover, is a sailor and no good can come from "dat ole devil, sea." Mat and Anna both understand that the sea is actually Chris's self and tell him so. Mat answers Chris's opposition to the marriage with: "Is it blaming the sea for your troubles ye are again, God help you?" And he goes on to accuse Chris of being afraid of the sea, as indeed he is—afraid of himself and his own responsibility. "The sea give you a clout once, knocked you down, and you're not man enough to get up for another, but lie there for the rest of your life howling bloody murder." (Act III, *Plays*, III, p. 48)

Anna, however, settles the controversy by telling Mat that she cannot marry him. He finally forces her to tell the truth about her past, to which he reacts as she foresaw. He curses her and stalks out to sign up on a boat. Chris's reaction is to run away from the situation—he, too, signs up for a voyage, explaining that that will be best for Anna. She will have his wages, and maybe "if dat ole davil gat me back she leave you alone den." Anna tries to show him his weakness (Act IV, *Plays*, III, p. 66): ". . . don't you see you're doing the same thing you've always done? Don't you see—(*But she sees the look of obsessed stubbornness on her father's face and gives it up helplessly.*)"

In the controversial conclusion of the play is additional evidence of O'Neill's double vision of life as suspended between hope and despair. Mat comes back and when Anna swears that she never loved any man before him, they are reconciled and plan to be married. Critics accused O'Neill of deliberately twisting the plot to achieve a happy ending, which, they said, was unconvincing. In a letter to *The New York Times*, O'Neill replied at length that the play has no ending; that behind this immediate solution of their problem, the characters' lives go on as always.

It would have been so obvious and easy . . . to have made my last act a tragic one. It could have been done in ten different ways, any one of them superficially right. But looking deep into the hearts of my people, I saw it couldn't be done. It would not have been true. They were not that kind. They would act in just the silly, immature, compromising way that I have made them act; and I thought that they would appear to others as they do to me, a bit tragically humorous in their vacillating weakness. (*The New York Times*, December 12, 1921)

So, indeed, we might add, appear the characters of *Beyond the Horizon* and *The Straw*. O'Neill adds that there "never was a more sentimental gesture of defiance at fate than that of Burke and Anna agreeing to wed." Fate, the sea of their weak, bewildered selves, remains to toss them still. The ending may be happy for Anna, but it is to Chris that O'Neill turns for the closing words of the play: "Fog, fog, fog, all bloody time. You can't see where you vas going, no. Only dat ole devil sea—she knows!"

The backdrop of sea and fog against which Anna Christie takes place not only symbolizes the "mystery behind existence," but hints also of the Jungian race memory or collective unconscious. Jung himself has called the sea "the symbol of the collective unconscious because it hides unsuspected depths under a reflecting surface." [8] O'Neill makes much of the fact that the sea is in the Christopherson blood; Chris tells Anna the long seafaring history of the family, who come from a village where all the men were sailors or fishermen. He is alarmed when he sees Anna responding to the spell as she feels it in the fog:

ANNA: (*After a pause—dreamily.*) Funny! I do feel sort of—nutty, tonight. I feel old.

CHRIS: (*Mystified*) Ole?

ANNA: Sure—like I'd been living a long, long time—out here in the fog. (*Frowning perplexedly.*) I don't know how to tell you yust what I mean. It's like I'd come home after a long visit away some place. It all seems like I'd been here before lots of times—on boats—in this same fog. (Act III, *Plays*, III, p. 28)

Evidence that O'Neill had the Jungian concept in mind here is particularly strong in view of the fact that he suggests it, certainly, in *The Hairy Ape*, with Yank's search for a past to which to belong, and makes it the keystone of *The Emperor Jones*, written in the same year (1920) as the completed version of *Anna Christie*.

All the searchers—Yank, Robert, Stephen, Chris—are bewildered wanderers in a fog of ignorance and illusion. They are seeking "to belong"—but to what? They cannot know the answer until they know themselves; but the self is what they have lost. Robert and Stephen make a virtue of necessity by proclaiming renunciation of the self the solution; actually, they are renouncing not the self, but the search for it. Their apparent discoveries are in fact evasions. Yank and Chris, too, have their evasions—the former in self-destruction, the latter in flight. They owe whatever blundering direction their lives may have to the tension between the hidden self and an image of it which has no definite shape for them. Each has a "tragic flaw" which blinds him to the self-image: the brutish unintelligence of Yank, the egotism, self-deception, and weakness of Robert, Stephen, and Chris. Yank's tragic flaw is insuperable except by death—he is himself a flaw—a kind of freak; the flaws of the other three might have been overcome by confronting and understanding the self, not by sacrificial self-denial alone.

While O'Neill has seen the search for identity as one of the impelling forces of life, he has also perceived that a lifetime spent in searching for self may be a "soul-stifling" struggle. Only on the stage, in the realm of drama, could the tragic fate of Yank, or Chris, or Robert, or Stephen, be conceived of as a celebration of life. What is celebrated is waste, incompletion, frustration—a struggle with nonexistent obstacles. We never completely solve the secret of identity nor resolve the conflicts between opposite aspects of the self—but the healthy human being manages to live with the unknowns and the opposites, and does not postpone forever, while he solves the riddle of self, the objective challenges life offers to human creativity.

In 1950, seven years after O'Neill had finished his last play, Karen Horney published her final book, *Neurosis and Human Growth,* subtitled *The Struggle toward Self-realization.* Regardless of the depth, correctness, or finality of Horney's theory, one cannot help being struck by the astonishing correspondence between her descriptions of neurotic types and the patterns of human behavior which appear in O'Neill's heroes. The direction of movement taken by these patterns—their development as well as their repetition—points unmistakably not only to O'Neill's conscious insight, but to his unconscious involvement with his heroes, his own struggle with problems similar to theirs.

Horney's concept helps explain both plays and playwright; but while her system describes and clarifies O'Neill's problem, it does not, of course, account for it.

Dr. Horney considers the "intrapsychic" struggle with self (the true *agon* of all O'Neill's work) the central conflict of all neurosis. She sees the struggle as arising from unconscious self-hatred—as Kierkegaard saw it—with the projection of an idealized image of the self as one of the neurotic solutions to self-hatred.

This neurotic process, as Dr. Horney makes clear, is perfectly parallel to that very process of striving for the infinite which accounts for all the forward movements of normal men. The difference lies in the neurotic's need to direct all his energy against his hated self, rather than against the outside world. The goal of therapy is therefore to find the source of the unconscious self-hatred and to overcome it, to lead the individual to acceptance of himself and to the realization of his potentialities as an active human being.

Horney distinguishes between three aspects of the self: The *actual* or *empirical* self is "an all-inclusive term for everything that a person is at a given time: body and soul, healthy and neurotic." (*Neurosis and Human Growth,* p. 158) The *ideal* self is an unattainable ideal image, set up in response to "tyrannic shoulds"—the compulsions of the self-hater to deny what he is and to become what he thinks he should be. This ideal is not based on what the neurotic really wants to become in his innermost or "real" self, but upon what he thinks is required of him. His concern with his relationship to this self-image is a kind of pride; he may be arrogant in thinking that he actually has attained his goal or he may be terribly ashamed that he has not. In either case, his pride—inflated or wounded—is neurotic, for it is concerned not with real qualities or capabilities, but with phantoms projected by his own mind. To be sure, neurotic pride may drive him forward to success, but its basis is unreal, and the whole man may crumble when, consciously or unconsciously, he perceives the truth.

The third and most vital of the selves is the *real* self— that which is not conceptualized as an image, but felt. In Horney's words it is "that alive, unique, personal center of ourselves; the only part that can, and wants to, grow." (*Neurosis and Human Growth*, p. 155) It is the self from which the neurotic has become estranged—alienated—by his self-hatred, and which he has deserted in pursuit of false self-images or masks. The effort of the real self to assert itself against the whole "pride system" (the struggle between divergent should-projected masks) is what Horney calls the "central neurotic conflict."

In O'Neill's plays the actual, empirical self of a given character is that composite which is readily perceived by the audience—his observable identity (name, trade, physical appearance, the dramatic situation in which he is found). This may, of course, be the self perceived consciously by the character also, as it appears to be, at least, for Yank at the beginning of *The Hairy Ape*. The ideal self is the character's projected image of what he *should be,* which he often confuses with what he *is*—this confusion, of course, resulting ultimately in conflict and disintegration. To clear up the confusion, to determine the nature and value of this ideal image, to reconcile conflicting images, and to search either in the masks themselves or beneath them for the *real* self: this is the complex motivation of O'Neill's protagonists.

In this present group of dramas, the leading characters are searching for the selves from which they have become alienated. Each has rejected that empirical self which the audience can see, as well as the real self, demonstrating their self-hatred in so doing. The result is the alienation which Horney considers one of the earliest symptoms of unconscious self-hatred, and therefore of neurosis, and which on O'Neill's stage takes the same form that it does in daily life—or in the psychiatric clinic. It manifests itself first as a kind of amnesia. In Horney's words: "All of what a person actually is or has, including even his connection of his present life with his past, the feeling for this continuity of his life, may be blotted out or dimmed out." Dr. Horney proceeds further with the definition:

At the core of this alienation from the actual self is a phenomenon that is less tangible although more crucial. It is the remoteness of the neurotic from his own feelings, wishes, beliefs, and energies. It is the loss of the feeling of being an active determining force in his own life. It is the loss of feeling himself as an organic whole. These in turn indicate an alienation from that most alive center of ourselves which I have suggested calling the *real self*. . . . It engenders the spontaneity of feelings, whether these be joy, yearning, love, anger, fear, despair. It also is the source of spontaneous interests and energies . . . ; the capacity to wish and to will; it is the part of ourselves that wants to expand and grow and to fulfill itself. (*Neurosis and Human Growth*, pp. 156–157)

On the basis of this definition, the plays in this group are studies in alienation—as indeed, basically, are all of O'Neill's plays. Even in the first experiments there were wanderers in the fog, searching for identity, and perfect examples of neurotic pride, in Keeney and in Mrs. Frazer.

Some of Horney's descriptions of the symptomatic behavior of sufferers from alienation are such strikingly accurate characterizations of Chris and Yank (of *The Hairy Ape*) as to merit full quotation here. This first excerpt is a portrait of Chris:

> In [the less conspicuous forms] of alienation from self. . . . there is no gross loss of identity and orientation, but the general capacity for conscious experience is impaired. There are for instance many neurotics who live as if they were in a fog. Nothing is clear to them. Not only thoughts and feelings but also other people, and the implications of a situation, are hazy. (*Neurosis and Human Growth*, p. 156)

And there is this:

> While the impairment or loss of the directive powers may be hidden, there is another insufficiency that is always clearly discernible, at least to the trained observer: *the faculty of assuming responsibility for self*. . . . Here again, as in other functions, pride has taken over responsibility and hounds him with condemnatory accusations when he fails to do the impossible. This then makes it close to impossible to assume the only responsibility that matters. This is, at bottom, no more but also no less than *plain, simple honesty about himself and his life*. It operates in three ways: a square recognition of his being as he is, without minimizing or exaggerating; a willingness to bear the consequences of his actions, decisions, etc., without trying to "get by" or to put the blame on others; the realization that it is up to him to do something about his difficulties without insisting that others, or fate, or time will solve them. . . . (*Neurosis and Human Growth*, pp. 168–169)

or, we might add, that "ole davil sea."

And here is Yank:

Finally, there are *active moves against* the real self, as expressed in self-hates. With the real self in exile, so to speak,
one becomes a condemned convict, despised and threatened
with destruction. The idea of being oneself becomes loath-
some and terrifying. . . . As a protection against this terror
the neurotic "makes himself disappear." He has an unconscious
interest in not having a clear perception of himself—in making
himself, as it were, deaf, dumb, and blind. . . . The factors
precipitating the feelings of unreality are usually severe in-
juries to pride together with an acute increase of self-contempt,
exceeding what is tolerable for the particular person. (*Neurosis and Human Growth,* pp. 160–161)

We recall that Yank's experience with Mildred has
wounded him in "the heart of his pride." Horney would
say that his was not a pride in his real self, but a neurotic
pride, and indeed we see evidence of it not only in the
complete destruction of his self-image by one word from
the girl, but also in his early exaggerated idea of his powers
and his refusal to accept consciously the spiritual and intellectual side of man because it is lacking in himself.
Even at his most confident, therefore, he was still alienated
from the totality of himself.

Robert of *Beyond the Horizon* and Stephen of *The
Straw,* are obviously also aliens from self, but the fact that
they find a conscious solution to their dilemma in self-
sacrifice brings to the fore a second phase of Horney's
theory which is vital in understanding O'Neill's work and
presents clues to the playwright's own character.

The neurotic must "protect himself from the disruptive
power of the conflict by finding pseudosolutions." (*Neuro-*

sis and Human Growth, p. 175) These solutions are, as it were, extreme caricatures of normal processes—a fact which makes them deceptive both to the neurotic himself and to the observer. "Leaving out more complex possibilities, the neurotic can feel himself as his glorified self, as his despised self, and at times (although this is mostly blocked out) as his true self." Since he experiences both the glorified and the despised selves he is bound to lose a knowledge of his real identity.

If these two ways of experiencing himself operate at the same time he must feel like two people pulling in opposite directions. And this indeed is the significance of the identification *in toto* with the two existing selves. There is not only a conflict, but a conflict of sufficient impact to tear him apart. (*Neurosis and Human Growth,* p. 189)

In order to ease the tension of this unbearable dichotomy, the neurotic may automatically and unconsciously identify himself with one or the other of the selves, thus achieving an apparent—but precariously temporary—integration. If he identifies with his ideal self, accepts what Horney calls "the expansive solution: the appeal of mastery," he may become arrogant, vindictive, tyrannical—acknowledging no equal nor superior in other people, and no error nor failing in himself. If, on the other hand, he identifies with his despicable self, the object of his self-hatred, he may become abject and submissive. He tends "to feel helpless, is compliant and appeasing, depends upon others and craves their affection." Horney calls this "the self-effacing solution: the appeal of love." And there is a third pseudosolution to the conflict of self: One may simply resign altogether from the struggle, picture one-self as an impassive observer invulnerable to human emotion, uninvolved in struggle, free. Horney terms this solution "resignation: the appeal of freedom."

Ruth, of *Beyond the Horizon,* finds her solution by resignation from the struggle "into that spent calm beyond the troubling of any hope." Larry, the "old philosopher" of *The Iceman Cometh,* will find a temporary freedom in detachment—until he sees its other face, despair.

The solution in self-effacement has been all too apparent in as early a play as *Servitude,* where the reader knows that Mrs. Frazer's negation of self will not last long—sooner or later her husband will feel her expansive drives again. Stephen renounces his egotism and finds himself; Robert, torn between scorn of the dreamer in himself and pride in him, finds a self-effacing solution in sacrifice. Robert, like Yank, finds the ultimate in self-effacement—death—his only solution to the problems of living.

The old, fanatical skipper of *Ile* and the early, arrogant Yank of *The Hairy Ape* find their answers in mastery —that solution of a Hitler, a Tamburlaine, an Ahab. And this is the theme of O'Neill's next group of plays, those whose protagonists are fanatics and extremists—brooking no acknowledgment of reality, no identification with their real selves, but finding their solutions to disintegration in a temporary and pitiful fusion with a false, impossible ideal image.

In 1920 O'Neill completed *Gold, The Emperor Jones,* and *Diff'rent,* and in the winter of 1921, *The First Man.* These plays are dominated by personalities who, like the searchers, are aliens from self; but they are not bewildered. They know, or think they know, exactly who they are and what they want. Fulfillment requires them to betray and destroy other human beings, but always in the spirit of a suffering Abraham forced to sacrifice a beloved son, for whom no ram appears. Too late, or never, the destroyer learns that the voice demanding slaughter was not God's or Fate's, but that of sheer hallucination. The voice came from be-

hind a hollow mask—his own false ego-image. In his ignorance or fear of the nothingness behind the mask, he is
desperately propelled toward integration with the mask
itself. At all costs he must become that grandiose, chi-
merical self-image. His monomania ignores the opposites
of life and of self and hurtles him on toward madness or
death.

The first of these proud self-deceivers is Bartlett, the
protagonist of *Gold*. He is a literary descendant of Keeney,
in *Ile*—a whaling skipper obsessed by a desire for wealth
which culminates in murder.

Bartlett and his men are shipwrecked on an island,
when, half-mad with thirst, they discover a chest of cheap
brass jewelry used for trading with the natives. The captain and two frenzied shipmates, Horne and Gates, convince themselves that the jewelry is genuine and that they
have discovered vast wealth. But the cook and cabin boy,
who have retained their sanity by means of a small hidden
supply of water, realize the jewelry is "junk" and make
the mistake of saying so. Although Bartlett forces them to
recant, they have now become suspect to him and to the
other men, who persuade themselves that the cook and
the cabin boy plan to steal the jewelry. As a rescue ship
approaches, Bartlett gives his tacit agreement to the murder and swift burial of the cook and cabin boy.

Bartlett returns home and outfits a ship for another
voyage to the "treasure island," keeping the purpose of the
voyage a secret from his family. The murders have been
preying on his conscience, but in his escape from reality
he has convinced his conscious self that he is innocent because he "spoke no word." His wife, sick and brought near
death by Bartlett's behavior, suspects his guilt and feels

that the voyage is a mission purporting some further evil. By threatening to take their only son with him, Bartlett forces her against her will to give her name to the ship— his guilt making him believe that his luck depends upon the ship's having the "name of a good woman." Bartlett's daughter, however, in sympathy with her mother, has her fiancé take the ship to sea while Bartlett is at the bedside of his dying wife.

A year later, after his wife's death, Bartlett, now insane, watches the sea, living only for the return of the schooner. News has arrived that it has been wrecked and sunk, but the old man clings to his delusion, with frequent hallucinations that the ship is moored in the harbor. Moreover, he has told his son, Nat, the story from his own mad point of view. Nat agrees that his father was right in allowing the murders and becomes drawn into Bartlett's delusions —sharing even his fixed idea that the ship has returned. When the daughter, Sue, sees that Nat has been virtually hypnotized by his father, that he seems "to give way to the stronger will," she cries out to Bartlett:

Stop, do you hear me! It's all mad! You're driving Nat mad too! (*As she sees her father hesitate, the wild light dying out of his eyes, she summons all her power to a fierce pleading.*) For my sake, Pa! For Ma's sake! Think of how she would feel if she were alive and saw you acting this way with Nat! Tell him! Tell him now—before me—tell him it's all a lie! (Act IV, *Plays,* II, p. 690)

At this crucial point, Bartlett is redeemed by the only value life has for him outside himself—the love of his son. At the moment that he acknowledges this love, he perceives the falsity of the self-conception to which he has dedicated his life. He tells Nat the truth, admitting that he gave his consent to the murder "in cold blood," and shows Nat the piece of jewelry he brought back from the island. Nat's pronouncement that the gold is false tears away the last remnant of the mask which Bartlett has shown to himself as a self-image, and he "groans and seems to shrink up and turn into a figure of pitiable weakness." (Act IV, *Plays*, II, p. 692) Nat, released from the power of his father's mania, comes to his senses, and Bartlett

uncovers his gray face on which there is now settling an expression of strange peace. . . . He slowly tears [the map of the island] into small pieces, seeming to grow weaker and weaker as he does so. Finally as he lets the fragments filter through his fingers, his whole frame suddenly relaxes. He sighs, his eyes shut, and sags back in his chair, his head bent forward limply on his chest. [He is dead.]

The ironic symbolism of the title of *Gold* reflects the falseness of a self-conception completely blinded to reality by pride, by the demands of the ego. The tenuous nature of such a self-relationship is shown in Bartlett's having with him a sample of the "gold" throughout all the deluded years, never daring to have it examined, just as he never dares to examine the reality of his responsibility for the murders. With or without the psychoanalytic tags of rationalization or wish-fulfillment, such self-deception has been a fatal flaw of tragic heroes from Oedipus to Willy Loman. Within the framework of Horney's theory of "neurotic pride," the psychiatric and the literary patterns become beautifully parallel.

Bartlett is the first of O'Neill's characters—except for his early prototype, Keeney—to find a pseudosolution to unconscious self-hatred in mastery. His pride in his real self is so deficient that he must compensate for it by the pride in a self-conception which does not and cannot really exist. As Horney points out, this is the psychological counterpart of all the Faust legends—the individual who sells his soul to the devil for a promise of unlimited powers, who sells the potentiality of a productive life for a chest of false gold. One cannot, of course, think of O'Neill's Bartlett without recalling again that other stricken skipper, Captain Ahab. The pattern is the same. The monomaniac spends his life pursuing an impossible and unreal goal in order to compensate for a mutilation of the self. The mutilation symbolizes to him all that is despicable in that "real" self which he has rejected for an imaginary portrait of Ahab as the miracle-worker, the great avenger. *Gold*, though it may be theatrical melodrama—a fantastic, spectacular pirate story for adults—is nevertheless the beginning of O'Neill's attempt to knit together the ancient and the modern tragic view of life. The hero usurps the prerogatives of Godhead and brings down upon himself the crushing Nemesis of reality, before which the grand illusion crumbles to dust and ashes.

As Bartlett is driven by his lust for gold, so the "Emperor Jones" is driven by his lust for power. Like Bartlett, Jones cannot rest until he has been united with and destroyed by an impossible, self-projected mask of himself as an absolute and invulnerable dictator. The story of the play is the gradual revelation to him of what lies behind the mask—the hollow evil in which his true self has long been lost. The terms of this revelation are those not only of O'Neill, but also of Jung.

O'Neill was always defensive, and with some justice, toward accusations like that made by Barrett Clark, that some of his plays were "expressed and patterned somewhat too precisely after Freud and Jung." O'Neill's answer to Clark was in part as follows:

Authors were psychologists, you know, and profound ones before psychology was invented. And I am no deep student of psychoanalysis. As far as I can remember, of all the books written by Freud, Jung, etc., I have read only four, and Jung is the only one of the lot who interests me. Some of his suggestions I find extraordinarily illuminating in the light of my own experience with hidden human motives.[1]

The "suggestion" which excited O'Neill in *The Emperor Jones* was Jung's fundamental premise—the existence and power of the collective unconscious. The mind of a given man contains ideas from the collective unconscious which come to him simply by virtue of his membership in the human race, as well as ideas inherited from his own specific race, tribe, and family. His mind contains, in addition, unconscious ideas and symbols arising from his unique personal situation to make up the structure of his personal unconscious. Finally, from this personal unconscious emerges his own consciousness, his ego.

The Emperor Brutus Jones (not Caesar, but Brutus) is an ex-Pullman porter who, through deception and corruption, has become emperor and possessor of great wealth on an island in the West Indies. The significance of the play lies not in the superficial narrative, which consists largely in a pursuit of Jones through the forest by the rebellious natives, but in the character of Jones, conveyed through a gradual breaking down of his conscious ego and the revelation of his personal and collective unconscious. Jones's hopeless flight through the forest is not from the natives at all, but from himself—the fundamental self from which his blind pride and its self-image have so long separated him, and which, inevitably, comes into its own. This is the primary symbolism of his movement through the forest in a circle, hypnotized by the rhythm of a drum beat and ending where he began. The progress of Jones is progress in self-understanding; it is the stripping off of the masks of self, layer by layer, just as bit by bit his "emperor's" uniform is ripped from his back, until at the end he must confront his destiny—himself—in nakedness.

As the play begins, Jones, attired in his gaudy emperor's costume, is boasting to Smithers, his cockney helper, of his rise to power. The record has been one of violence and trickery, murder and cheating, but Jones has arrived. He has allowed no obstacle to come between him and his self-image, but now at the moment of integration, dissolution is imminent. Jones has gone too far in his exploitation of the natives; they are at the point of rebellion—have, in fact, already planned to depose the "emperor"—and he must flee for his life. Jones has convinced the natives, however, that only a silver bullet can kill him (thinking that they would hardly be able to find silver on the island) and has forged a silver bullet for himself—the sixth, and last, in his gun—in case he must kill himself before the natives get to him. In doing so, Jones has already given the natives the real key to his destruction—the self and its pride: "I tells 'em dat's cause I'm de on'y man in de world big enuff to git me." (Scene I, *Plays*, III, p. 179)

Nowhere in O'Neill's work is his theatrical skill more evident than in Jones's flight through the jungle to the drumbeat which begins at normal pulse rhythm, growing faster and faster, louder and louder. As Jones proceeds, lost in the forest he had thought he knew so well, he is confronted with one ghost after another from his past, each representing an aspect of himself or a hidden motive for his past action, and each of which can be dispelled only by his firing one of his six precious bullets. First appear his "little formless fears," then his guilt, in two visions—the ghost of the Negro, Jeff, for whose murder in a gambling fight he was sent to prison, and the ghost of the guard whom he killed in his escape from prison. These three episodes, stemming from fear and guilt, come from Jones's "personal unconscious," while the three following ones emerge from his "collective unconscious."

He must fire his fourth and fifth bullets to dispel the vision of a slave auctioneer who he thinks is about to sell him from the block. By this time Jones is naked and exhausted; he lies down to rest and is surrounded by a group of savages—his ancestors—whose voices, beginning with a low, melancholy murmur, rise in a desperate wail which Jones first tries to shut from his ears, then joins, his voice rising above the others. The scene of this final vision is laid at a stone altar near a tree—sexual as well as religious symbols. Jones has shed the last layer of his civilized outward self and has gone back to the dark, primitive world of the unconscious, where physical and spiritual birth are one. When he has thrown himself at the foot of the altar to pray, he realizes that he has returned to the clearing where he entered the forest; he is back where his journey began. And here the rites of exorcism must take place.

A Congo witch doctor enters and begins a wild dance in which Jones joins:

The whole spirit and meaning of the dance has entered into him, has become his spirit. Finally the theme of the pantomime halts on a howl of despair, and is taken up again in a note of savage hope. There is a salvation. The forces of evil demand sacrifice. . . . Jones seems to sense the meaning of this. It is he who must offer himself for sacrifice. (Scene VII, *Plays*, III, p. 201)

Evil has been his god, and he has sacrificed all other values to it; now it demands his life. The witch doctor summons from the river a terrifying crocodile, whose glittering eyes fasten upon Jones. He stares at them in paralyzed fascination at first, then, shouting defiantly, "De silver bullet! You don't git me yit!" fires at the crocodile, which, with the witch doctor, disappears, as Jones falls to the ground. He lies there, "his arms outstretched, whimpering with fear as the throb of the tom-tom fills the silence about him with a somber pulsation, a baffled but revengeful power." (Scene VII, *Plays*, III, p. 202) From the symbolism of the dance and the use of the silver bullet, we know that the evil represented by the crocodile is the evil of the self, that in killing it Jones has killed himself—at least, that distorted image of the self which was his life motivation. He has performed the justice demanded by the dance.

The play might have ended here, for Jones is, in effect, dead; but O'Neill adds a final scene, important for the portrayal of Jones as a tragic hero who died as he lived, with a kind of grandeur, false though it was. It returns us to the conscious level of experience, the realism with which the play opens. The natives have shot Jones with a silver bullet which they made from money—an appropriate symbol of the destruction of self by its own pride and greed. The

tragic pull between the selves no longer exists, nor, of
course, does life. The integration has cost Jones everything, but he got what he wanted; and as Smithers says in
the closing lines of the play, "Silver bullets! gawd blimey,
but yer died in the 'eighth o'style, any'ow!"

In his use of symbols in *The Emperor Jones* O'Neill acknowledged, as do most modern authors, the validity of
Jung's theory that great literature strikes a responsive
chord in all men because its central metaphors can be
traced to archetypal images buried in the unconscious
mind of humanity. In Jung's words:

> The secret of artistic creation and of the effectiveness of art
> is to be found in a return to the state of *participation mystique*
> —to that level of experience at which it is man who lives, and
> not the individual, and at which the weal or woe of the single
> human being does not count, but only human existence. That
> is why every great work of art is objective and impersonal,
> but none the less profoundly moves us each and all.[2]

The pitfall for the artist, however, may lie—as in some
of the later plays it does for O'Neill—in his very awareness
of this truth. Open-eyed, conscious manipulation of archetypal symbols may achieve only a strained and artificial
objectivity—a too-explicit cry for the immortal and the
universal. Wider public knowledge of these symbols has
also weakened their effectiveness; many images which
used to move us profoundly for reasons which we did not
quite understand have now become artistic platitudes.
Everybody knows about Oedipus. The secret, obviously,
is not in the symbol, but in the skillful adaptation. In *The
Emperor Jones,* O'Neill achieves a dynamic synthesis of
symbol and dramatic action. The focus of the play is in-

ward, but it is consistently inward, and the final revelation is the logical climax of revelations which have gone before. However, as always in O'Neill's best plays, outward reality has the first and last word. Brutus Jones emerges as unforgettably himself: a gigantic figure brought low by the very forces which exalted him; universal, but not Man; individual, but not Eugene O'Neill.

Diff'rent, the third in this group of "extremist" plays, is a minor melodrama in itself but provides an important thematic link between O'Neill's early and his later concepts. The heroine, Emma Crosby, is another fanatic, a neurotic of the type referred to by Horney (for reasons which will become obvious) as "the perfectionist." She is interesting, too, as a New England forerunner of Tennessee Williams's thwarted Southern heroine.

Emma is a victim of Puritanism combined with notions of chivalric love drawn from romantic novels. As a young girl, Emma rejects her faithful suitor, Caleb, because he falls short of the ideal lover she has found in books. He is a vigorous man, a sea captain, who admits that once on a voyage to the South Seas he was seduced by a native girl. Emma had expected Caleb to be "diff'rent" from other men—to be pure and perfect—and cannot forgive him for a transgression which O'Neill makes more than excusable by the circumstances. Like many of O'Neill's women—notably Margaret in *The Great God Brown*—Emma cannot love the real, whole man, but only her illusory conception of him. When that no longer exists, neither does her love.

Then Emma, at forty, with all the passion of accumulated frustration, falls in love with a boy of twenty, a wastrel who deceives her. Caleb, who has waited all these years in the hope that Emma will marry him if he proves his love by remaining true to her (and thereby also becoming a victim of frustration), discovers her passion for the boy. His equally false picture of Emma as an eternal virgin is shattered, and in disappointment and disillusionment he hangs himself. When Emma discovers that the young scoundrel wants only her money and that Caleb is dead, she too determines upon suicide, calling to Caleb to wait for her.

The theme of *Diff'rent* is one which will become a chief source of power in O'Neill's later work. Up to this point he has always thrown reality and illusion into conflict. He has equated reality with outward facts and inward alienation from self, and illusion with false values and a false self-image. This remains always his basic distinction, but in *Diff'rent* O'Neill widens the concept of reality to include biological—here sexual—necessity, and that of illusion to include repression of sexual drives. This treatment of repression is still closely related to the concept of illusion as pride, for denial of sexual love implies an inability to reach outside one's own ego. Emma's real flaw is not a lack of desire for love, but self-centeredness and prudish guilt. Nature is the reality which avenges itself upon her egotism. Nature has not only been thwarted but insulted by the Puritan sense of sin, which distorts the desire of normal love to lust. In O'Neill's subsequent work the vengeance of nature upon Puritanic arrogance becomes a dominant motif.

Another character who tries to subject the demands of nature to his own egotistical illusions is Curtis Jayson, hero of *The First Man*. Curtis is a consummate escapist whose life history began with romantic idealism, but the ideal becomes an impossible self-image which he is doomed to pursue forever. He never discovers "the secret of sacrifice" or acceptance of the very tragic opposites he tries to escape. He can see nothing beyond the limits of his own ego-image. Everything he loves is a projection of himself; every action drives him blindly on toward the realization of a self-conception which he thinks means his salvation, but which in reality means destruction for himself and the woman who loves him.

Jayson is a successful anthropologist, dedicated to his work. As the play opens he has reached the climax of his career with an opportunity to go to Asia to excavate what may be the ruins of "the first man." Curtis's extreme devotion to anthropology followed the sudden death of his children. His wife's explanation of his motives is the key to Curtis's character:

MARTHA: We were real lunatics for a time. And then when we'd calmed down enough to realize—how things stood with us—we swore we'd never have children again—to steal away their memory. It wasn't what you thought—romanticism— that set Curt wandering—and me with him. It was a longing to lose ourselves—to forget. He flung himself with all his power into every new study that interested him. He couldn't keep still, mentally or bodily—and I followed. He needed me—then—so dreadfully!

BIGELOW: And is it that keeps driving him on now?

MARTHA: Oh, no. He's found himself. His work has taken the place of the children. (Act I, *Plays*, II, p. 557)

For Martha, however, the work has not been enough. She has been deeply involved in it but finds now that she needs more, that she wants to have children. Since she knows that Curt will be away on his search for "the first man" for five years, she has deliberately become pregnant, hoping that he will understand and be happy for her —will forget their original oath not to have any more children. When she tells Curt, however, he is angry and horrified, since he had arranged for her to go with him. His behavior reveals that his anger comes not from a conviction that she is desecrating the memory of the dead children, but from his own selfish desire to have her accompany him on the trip; he feels she is indispensable to him. His possessive love for her cannot tolerate the thought of having to share her affection with a child:

. . . Oh, Martha, why do you have to bring this new element into our lives at this late day? Haven't we been sufficient, you and I together? Isn't that a more difficult, beautiful happiness to achieve than—children? Everyone has children. Don't I love you as much as any man could love a woman? Isn't that enough for you? Doesn't it mean anything to you that I need you so terribly—for myself, for my work—for everything that is best and worthiest in me? Can you expect me to be glad when you propose to introduce a stranger who will steal away your love, your interest—who will separate us and deprive me of you! . . . (Act II, *Plays*, II, p. 586)

Slowly Martha realizes his egotism and narrowness, his delusion that his work is what is "best and worthiest" in him. But not until he proposes that she have an abortion does she begin to understand that he has never really loved her except as a projection of himself. "Yes," she says, "you love me. But who am I? You don't know." (Act II, *Plays*, II, p. 588)

The plot has been complicated by the fact that Curtis's

family, the proud "first family" of the community, have suspected Martha of an affair with Bigelow; and from Curt's attitude toward the child they deduce that the father is actually Bigelow. Fearful all along of disgrace to the family name, they have been persecuting Martha, but Curt has not even noticed her struggle nor guessed his family's suspicion. Martha suffers agony in labor, and before the child is born Curtis knows that his wife will die. At first he is desperate, guilt-tormented, because he thinks she has felt only his hatred of the child rather than his love for her. Before she dies, however, she begs him in a whisper to forgive her, and, characteristically, he interprets this in the light of his own egotism. "But she loved me again—only me—I saw it in her eyes. She had forgotten —it." (Act III, *Plays*, II, p. 602)

The child whom Curt hates is a boy, as Martha wanted. Curt has determined never to look at him and to go on his trip, return to his work, "for only in it will I find Martha again." In spite of Bigelow's pleadings, he refuses to face the fact that the real Martha is in the child, that only if he becomes reconciled to his son will he be true to her. He finally sees a glimmering of this idea when his family force him to acknowledge the child to allay their suspicions that he is not the father. Even then, although he promises to return, he still sees the child as a projection of himself— just as he saw the mother. "When he's old enough I'll teach him to know a big, free life. . . . Martha shall live again for me in him." (Act IV, *Plays*, II, p. 618)

And he departs on his search for *The First Man*—himself.

This conception of Curtis as "the first man" and Martha as "the first woman" is another which relates this play—

and others to follow—to the psychology of Jung. The characters of Curtis and Martha are stereotypes which, like many of O'Neill's men and women, correspond closely to the Jungian male and female archetypal images, the *animus* and *anima.* In extremely general and oversimplified terms the concept is this: Each man has in his unconscious the soul-image of a woman, the *anima,* who represents some of the man's own suppressed feminine characteristics. Comparably, each woman has a male soul-image—the *animus*—representing her own suppressed masculinity. The characteristics of these images are the archetypal male and female characteristics: The male is, like the *yang* of Eastern philosophy, the "Spiritual Principle" of the universe, while the female, the *yin,* is the "Physical Principle."

In his effort to make his characters symbolic, O'Neill has often confined them to almost diagrammatical representations of the Jungian typical male, intellectually creative, idealistic, egotistical, and aggressive (like Curtis), and the typical female, physically creative, realistic, unselfish, and passive, who is as much a mother to her husband as she is a wife. She appears in many of the archetypal forms which Jung says are images of the *anima;* she is an Earth Mother representing the processes and cycles of nature (Cybel, in *The Great God Brown;* Mrs. Fife, in *Dynamo;* Abbie, in *Desire under the Elms*) or a kind of Faustian Marguerite (Beatriz, of *The Fountain;* Kukachin, of *Marco Millions,* and Margaret, of *The Great God Brown*). She has various degrees of the redemptive power; Martha, for example, with all her earthiness and realism, could have been Curtis's salvation if his egotism had ever allowed him to love her unselfishly. It is impossible to know, of course, exactly to what extent O'Neill drew upon the actual Jungian symbols. In broad outline these characterizations are commonplaces of literature and drama; suggestions of them pervade the work of Ibsen and Strindberg, the important early influences upon O'Neill. Nevertheless, the close similarity of many of O'Neill's characterizations and symbols to the Jungian concepts is more than coincidental, even though we accept them simply as illuminations of the playwright's own "experience with hidden human motives." O'Neill's literal acceptance of these archetypes suggests limitations in that experience and a certain immaturity in his entire view of the man-woman relationship which becomes increasingly clear in his work.

All of O'Neill's extremists are represented in Horney's varied list of types of expansive neurotics, but in Bartlett, Jones, and Jayson, O'Neill matched perfectly Horney's description of the "arrogant-vindictive" type:

His main motivating force in life is his need for vindictive triumph. . . . Even though in others the impact of the need for vengeance and triumph can be poignant, it usually is kept within limits by three factors: love, fear, and self-preservation. Only if these checks are temporarily or permanently malfunctioning can the vindictiveness involve the total personality —thereby becoming a kind of integrating force, as in Medea —and sway it altogether in the one direction of vengeance and triumph. (*Neurosis and Human Growth*, p. 198)

Swayed as they are in the "direction of vengeance and triumph," Bartlett and Jones are prevented from achieving ultimate victory by the final reassertion of the "checks"— for Bartlett, love, for Jones, self-preservation. They can find no lasting integration and live; for when the prideful

mask falls off—when the gold is proved false and the crocodile is dead—there is nothing left. In the pursuit of the
mask the real self has been irretrievably lost, rejected and
finally destroyed by unconscious self-hatred. Of all the
extremists, Curtis Jayson is the only one who keeps his
false integration, whose mask never falls away.

Curtis will use the imaginary "injustice" done him in the
death of his children as excuse for eternal vindictiveness
against the world, reality in general, and, unconsciously,
against himself. But while he is cruel and self-centered on
one hand, on the other Curtis is a sensitive romanticist and
idealist, a little boy longing for love and for a mother. We
have met him in O'Neill's work before, and will see him
again. As Robert or Chris or Stephen he was a "little boy
lost," but as Curtis he has found a second mask and from
now on will be torn between the two. He will be affectionate, supersensitive, poetic; he will also be arrogant, cruel,
tortured by his own disintegration—and despicable.

The extremists all achieve a kind of union with the aggressive mask, but theirs is no more a real or final answer
to the problem of self than that of the searchers, who find
a late and tentative integration in the submissiveness of
sacrifice. What then is the real solution? How can man live
without identity, in a world of opposite masks? Without
certainty, in a world of opposite values? O'Neill found
what was for him the answer during the next ten years,
the most productive of his life. It is the great discovery
made by the "finders."

Juan Ponce de Leon [*sic*], hero of *The Fountain*, is the first of "the finders." In his character O'Neill announces the theme of the entire series of plays written between 1921 and 1927. *The Fountain* gives the imaginary version of Ponce de León's search for the Fountain of Youth. Amid all the pseudo-historical intrigue of the plot, the real action of the play unfolds in the progress of Juan from soldier to poet, from cynical militarist to devout believer in "eternal becoming."

In the opening scenes Juan is an aggressive, greedy young soldier of fortune, who has suppressed the poet in himself. The woman who loves him, and whom he has rejected, warns him, "You will go far, soldier of iron—and dreamer. God pity you if those selves should ever clash." That clash, of course, is the central dramatic conflict of the play.

The latent poet in Juan is suggested symbolically in the character of his friend, Luis, the minstrel whose song is a choral refrain—repeated throughout the play with variations—commenting on the action and stating the theme of the play:

> Love is a flower
> Forever blooming.
> Life is a fountain
> Forever leaping
> Upward to catch the golden sunlight,
> Striving to reach the azure heaven;
> Failing, falling,
> Ever returning
> To kiss the earth that the flower may live.
>> (Part I, Sc. i, *Plays*, I, p. 384)

The young Juan rejects this philosophy with a flippant, "Charming, sir Poet, but a lie. . . ." Hungry for action, wealth, and fame, he sails with Columbus on the voyage that was to end with the discovery of the New World. Only Columbus aboard the ship is guided by faith or idealism; the others are motivated by nothing higher than greed for power and gold. The ship's company consists equally of priests and soldiers, representative of a Church and State which share the same imperialistic motives. Juan has convinced himself that he, at least, is not en-

tirely selfish: He wants glory and gold not only for himself, but for Spain.

Twenty years later, through his ruthlessness, political
skill, and luck, Juan has realized his ambitions. But now
the old aims seem hollow to him and his victories meaningless. As the aging governor of Puerto Rico, he has lost
all sense of devotion to Spain and conquest but has found
nothing to take its place. He has become a passive, disillusioned victim of the intrigue of the Church which attempts
to force him from his position. But upon the arrival from
Spain of Beatriz, the beautiful daughter of the woman
who loved him in his youth, Juan is reawakened to action.
The old man falls in love with Beatriz; his desperate desire
to become young again leads him on a fanatical search for
the Fountain of Youth. He places his hope now in a magi-
cal power in nature itself and in youth and love—which
before he rejected for military glory. ". . . I believe in
Nature. Nature is part of God. She can perform miracles.
. . . Let me be damned forever if Nature will only grant
me youth upon this earth again!" (Part II, Sc. vi, *Plays*,
I, pp. 421–422)

Following his mad hope, Juan allows himself to be led
by vengeful Indians to a spring where the Indians have
set a trap for him and his followers. As Juan kneels beside
the spring which he believes to be the Fountain of Youth,
he is hit by an Indian arrow and left for dead. In a semi-
conscious state he has a vision in which he makes his great
discovery.

From a mist rising around the spring appears the figure
of a woman who seems to represent Death, but as she steps
aside, the voice of Beatriz sings the life song of the first
part of the play, and a fountain rises from the spring, in

which Beatriz appears. Juan calls to her, but she ignores him and steps aside, as the figures of a Chinese poet, a Moor, an American Indian, and Luis, the poet-monk, arise in the fountain and join hands. The figures disappear as the song of Beatriz resumes, and Juan cries out as the song ends:

The ghosts are gone. What is the answer to their riddle? I am no poet. I have striven for what the hand can grasp. What is left when Death makes the hand powerless? (Part III, Sc. x, *Plays*, I, p. 441)

His answer comes as "Faith," when the four figures appear again as priests, each carrying the symbol of his religion. Slowly, however, as the figures disappear, Juan realizes their meaning: "All faiths—they vanish—are one and equal —within—(*awe and reverence creeping into his voice*) What are you, Fountain? That from which all life springs and to which it must return—God! Are all dreams of you but the one dream?" This is still not enough for him. He calls again for Youth—and is answered by Beatriz's voice singing:

Death is a mist
Veiling sunrise.

Instead of Youth, Old Age in the form of an old woman appears. At first Juan resists, but as she beckons to him he goes to her. As he touches her hands, "her mask of age disappears. She is Beatriz." Then Juan has his final revelation, which comes to him only at the moment of the acceptance of old age: "Beatriz! Age—Youth—They are the

same rhythm of eternal life!" The figure which represented
Death in the first vision reappears unmasked with the face
of Beatriz.

> I see! Fountain Everlasting, time without end! Soaring flame
> of the spirit transfiguring Death! All is within! All things dis-
> solve, flow on eternally! O aspiring fire of life, sweep the
> dark soul of man! Let us burn in thy unity! (*Beatriz'
> voice rises triumphantly*)
> VOICE: God is a flower
>   Forever blooming
>   God is a fountain
>   Forever flowing.
>
>   . . . .
>
> JUAN: O God, Fountain of Eternity, Thou art the All in One,
> the One in All—the Eternal Becoming which is Beauty!
> (Part III, Sc. x, *Plays*, I, pp. 441–442)

After his revelation Juan lives on for a short while, in
"the calm of deep spiritual serenity." He becomes reconciled to his own inevitable age and death, and gives his
blessing to Beatriz and her young lover—Juan's nephew,
and a youthful version of himself. Death comes to him as
the young couple sing the fountain song, and Juan cries:
". . . I am that song! One must accept, absorb, give back,
become oneself a symbol! Juan Ponce de Leon is past! He
is resolved into the thousand moods of beauty that make
up happiness. . . . Oh, Fountain of Eternity, take back
this drop, my soul!"

Juan has spent his life searching in the outward world
for that unity which could be found only in himself—"All
is within." He has attempted to escape time and change,
only to discover that the secret of life is in acceptance and

active fulfillment of these. In his vision he sees that the solution to conflict within the self is not to be found in any one sectarian faith, in love, or in nature, but in the oneness of all these as they are symbolized in the mind by analogy to one another. The fountain is the deep-lying, unconscious spring of spontaneous emotion, of creativity, of value without paralyzing question. It is the equivalent in mind of the fecund cycles of nature and therefore expresses itself in natural symbols. When Juan recognizes the relationship between the flower that dies so that another may bloom, and the youth and old age cycle of Beatriz (and later, of himself), he has placed man back into the context of the natural world from which he was alienated in *The Hairy Ape*. Suffering and death now have the same meaning for human life as they have for nature; they are inevitable components of process and growth. The fountain strives upward but is constantly

> Failing, falling,
> Ever returning
> To kiss the earth that the flower may live.

O'Neill had met this philosophy in various sources—in his reading of Lao-tse, of Nietzsche, Strindberg, Jung, Schopenhauer. He was to examine it from many points of view, to plunge into it and develop it and test it from his own experience.

The Fountain is a failure as drama for many reasons, but chiefly because it depends too heavily upon abstraction and revelation. It is actually a fantasy, demanding just the lightness of touch and the poetic skill which O'Neill lacked. Here, feeling becomes bombast and poetry a crude imitation of Waley's translations from the Chinese. Nevertheless, the water of the fountain flows through and animates the six plays which follow, beginning with *Welded.*

Welded (1922–24) is a study of the marriage of two egoists—"welded," rather than wedded, by a mutual dependency which they both fight. Just as Juan sought a union of youth and age, so Michael and Eleanor Cape look for a solution to the ambivalent love and hate, pride and humility of their relationship. The lovers, a successful playwright and an actress, are described in the stage directions as appearing in separate circles of light which, "like auras of egoism, emphasize and intensify Eleanor and Michael throughout the play. There is no other lighting. The two other people and the rooms are distinguishable only by the light of Eleanor and Michael." (Act I, *Plays,* II, p. 443)

Both characters are torn by a need for freedom and self-fulfillment on one hand, and a need for love on the other. Their mutual dread of being possessed by or absorbed in each other leads to a series of battles, culminating in a final quarrel and the decision to "kill" the love which binds them to each other. Their attempt to do so is a failure, and the couple come back together determined to accept their relationship as inevitable. Pride may be their sin, but it is also their redemption; it represents the separate personality each must be in order to live. The pain and possessiveness of love are only the opposite masks of its joy and fulfillment, parts of the whole, parts of "unity." In Michael's words:

And we'll torture and tear, and clutch for each other's souls!

—fight—fail and hate again—(*he raises his voice in aggressive triumph*) but!—fail *with pride*—with joy!

. . . .

. . . with you I become a whole, a truth! Life guides me back through the hundred million years to you. It reveals a beginning in unity that I may have faith in the unity of the end! (Act III, *Plays*, II, p. 488)

Welded is at best an interesting—and often deeply moving—attempt to dramatize a neurotic problem in the form of a morality play, to make a sick relationship understandable in universal terms. The characters are familiar archetypes—Michael, the tormented creative spirit, and Eleanor, the earthy realist who objects to Michael's conception of the ideal marriage as one "consummated at the altar rather than the kitchen range." Eleanor is after all civilized, and somewhat masculine in her need for independence and a successful career, so in order to complete the picture of "Woman" as the passive, powerfully docile source of physical creation, O'Neill has added another archetype who reappears in later plays. She is the prostitute whom Michael visits when he tries to annihilate his love for Eleanor. A prototype of Cybel in *The Great God Brown* she is the Earth Mother who accepts life as it is and men as they are and offers them what comfort she can. Her attitude toward her own miserable past is, "You got to laugh. You got to loin to like it."

Welded moves slowly, is mostly talk, and depends heavily upon the exclamation point to communicate intensity of feeling. Its message of inward struggle and resolution requires explication as well as projective techniques on the stage. In experimenting with expressionistic symbols

O'Neill used others besides the auras of egoism. The most interesting is that of the curtain scene, directions for which read as follows:

(He moves close to her and his hands reach out for hers. For a moment as their hands touch they form together one cross. Then their arms go about each other and their lips meet.) (Act III, *Plays,* II, pp. 488–489)

In this traditionally connotative blending of sexual and religious imagery O'Neill was trying to convey the essence of *Welded.* The passion on the cross unites within itself the pain and sacrifice demanded by love, and the resurrection is love itself.

Welded introduces for the first time in O'Neill's work another conflict, probably biographical in implication, which was to haunt his plays for a quarter century. Love between the sexes becomes man's greatest hope and his greatest threat. It conquers loneliness and the sterility of egotistical isolation, but also, as some of the existentialists have said, it is the lovers' mutual attempt to rob each other of freedom. Here is the same ambivalence which dominates Strindberg's work, but where Strindberg is negative, O'Neill is positive—or, at least, tries to be. His later heroes accept the duality as Michael does when he calls love "the insult we swallow as the price of life."

It is one thing, however, to accept the insult as a challenge, and quite another to lose oneself completely in the lover; to use "love" as a pretext for masochistic self-denial. This kind of love-relationship destroys the soul of the hero of *All God's Chillun Got Wings* (1923). He is Jim Harris, a Negro who marries a white ex-prostitute, Ella, whom he worships. The two have known each other since childhood, but only when Ella is sick and defeated by life does she consent to marry Jim. The marriage is to her—in spite of her gratitude to Jim—a symbol of her final degradation. Slowly her hatred of her husband grows and with it her guilt. At all costs she must establish her superiority over him. She does so by destroying his self-confidence so that he is incapable of passing the bar examination for which he has been studying.

Of course, Ella alone could not have shattered Jim. From the very opening of the play he reveals an unconscious hatred of the Negro in himself, and, therefore, of himself. He has deliberately renounced his hated self in order to attain an impossible self-image. Marrying Ella and becoming a lawyer are for Jim part of the unconscious longing to achieve what he thinks it means to be "white." His drives are what Horney calls "tyrannic shoulds," and his fear that he can never fulfill these demands makes him crawl in constant apology to himself and society.

To consider *All God's Chillun* a race-relations play is to be misled. O'Neill as always is interested in social forces only when they represent inner psychological forces. Black and white are at war in this play, but within the characters as well as between them. Jim has not been made a slave to white society, and society cannot cure his illness. He is his own and passion's slave. Here is his proposal of marriage to Ella:

I don't ask you to love me—I don't dare to hope nothing like that—I don't want nothing—only to wait—to know you like me —to be near you—to keep harm away . . . to serve you—to lie

at your feet like a dog that loves you—to kneel by your bed
like a nurse that watches over you sleeping—to preserve and
protect and shield you from evil and sorrow—to give my life
and my blood and all the strength that's in me to give you
peace and joy—to become your slave!—yes, be your slave—
your black slave that adores you as sacred! (*He has sunk to
his knees. In a frenzy of self-abnegation, as he says the last
words he beats his head on the flagstones.*) (Act I, Sc. iii, *Plays*,
II, p. 318)

The conflict reaches a climax when Ella's neurosis becomes madness. In her unleashed hatred, she stabs at
the African mask which has dominated the action from the
walls of Jim's home. Jim finally understands and faces the
situation with a moment of primitive vindictiveness when
he calls Ella "You devil; you white devil woman." Then,
as usual, he relents. Ella, now secure in her knowledge that
she has ruined him, regresses to the childhood world in
which she and Jim were friends and equals, knowing no
difference but color: ". . . and I'll put shoe blacking on
my face and pretend I'm black and you can put chalk
on your face and pretend you're white just as we used to
do. . . ." Now that Ella is the helpless invalid, the child
who needs his protection rather than a threatening alien
force, he accepts her affirmatively as his destiny:

(*Jim suddenly throws himself on his knees and raises his shining eyes, his transfigured face*) Forgive me, God—and make
me worthy! Now I see your Light again! Now I hear your
voice! (*He begins to weep in an ecstasy of religious humility*)
Forgive me, God, for blaspheming You! Let this fire of burning
suffering purify me of selfishness and make me worthy of the
child you send me for the woman You take away! (Act II, Sc.
iii, *Plays*, II, p. 342)

Jim has found his "wings." This is his revelation of order and meaning in the universe; he has hope now, and direction for his life. O'Neill well knew that the revelation was a delusion and the hope was hopeless. Jim has found a pseudosolution to the search for a lost self in submission—in renouncing the self that he thinks he can never find nor be. This ending is right and inevitable for this play, perfectly consistent with the portrait of Jim.

But Jim is no tragic hero and this is no tragic "epiphany" or self-recognition. It is rather a travesty of the resurrection implied in true tragedy. For the order which Jim temporarily disrupted (his slavery to Ella, his aspiration to "whiteness") is not a real order—not inevitable or meaningful outside his own sick mind. Jim's acceptance of this order as his destiny is a gesture just as inconclusive and sentimental as the defiance of fate by the characters in *Anna Christie*. Jim thinks he has found himself by losing himself, but he has only succeeded in losing himself forever. He has found what he wanted—a groveling, masochistic humility from which he will never be forced to rise again. The struggle is over and the antagonist, the unconscious mind, is the victor.

If Jim's mystical view of his destiny is a mistaken rationalization, if the fate decreed by the powerful inner world is often a delusion, where is one to seek for moral order? *Marco Millions* (1923–25) proposes an answer, echoing the spirit of *The Fountain*. *Marco Millions* is a diffuse pageant of the pull between the dual forces of mysticism and materialism, the inner and the outer world. Marco Polo is the extroverted materialist, Kukachin the introverted mystic, and Kublai Kaan must reconcile the two in himself.

Marco, together with his merchant uncles, is treated satirically throughout the play. Like Juan and some of his other prototypes, Marco begins life as a poet. Unlike them, however, he conquers this youthful tendency successfully and permanently, and becomes a brash Western Babbitt, intent on exploiting the resources of the East. Marco is never conscious that Kukachin, the sensitive granddaughter of the ruler, Kublai Kaan, loves him and dies of her love. Kukachin's death song expresses the mystical or inner justification of her fate: "Say this, I loved and died. Now I am love and live. And living have forgotten. And loving can forgive." (Prologue, *Plays*, II, p. 352) She has gone beyond desire, back to that primal unity in which no ego is a separate entity, no "self" exists, where opposites are one and all is at peace.

Kublai Kaan, her grandfather, has found no such peace. At first he shows toward Marco amused tolerance, then disgust, and finally, when he sees Marco's power over Kukachin, anger and grief. In his first bitterness the Kaan is almost persuaded that the values of the materialistic West are the true ones:

My hideous suspicion is that God is only an infinite, insane energy which creates and destroys without other purpose than to pass eternity in avoiding thought. Then the stupid man becomes the perfect Incarnation of Omnipotence and the Polos are the true children of God. (Act III, Sc. i, *Plays*, II, p. 426)

After the death of Kukachin, however, the Kaan seeks the answer in mysticism, in faith in some contemplative realm beyond conflict, into which he can be absorbed. But his search for a mystic absolute is doomed to failure. Only the passive, withdrawn, and saintly sage can suspend all human feeling in contemplation of the "Tao of Heaven." The "Tao of man" is the "way" of every active human being who must embrace the realities of the outward world as well as those of the inward, and must see them both as aspects of the "eternal becoming." The final scene develops this concept and adds dimension to the character of the Kaan. When the body of Kukachin is placed before him in the court, the Kaan questions the priests of each cult—Taoist, Confucian, Buddhist, Moslem—as to the meaning of the finality of death. (Act III, Sc. ii, *Plays*, II, p. 434)

KUBLAI: . . . Priest of Tao, will you conquer death by your mystic Way?
PRIEST OF TAO: (*bowing his head in submission—fatalistically*) Which is the greater evil, to possess or to be without? Death is.

The other priests echo the submissiveness and acquiescence of the Taoist, and the chorus of populace begin to weep. The Kaan himself weakens for a moment; then, when the people address him as the "Son of Heaven," he utters his own prayer for them to follow:

. . . be proud of life! Know in your heart that the living of life can be noble! Know that the dying of death can be noble! Be exalted by life! Be inspired by death! . . . Contain the harmony of womb and grave within you! Possess life as a lover —then sleep requited in the arms of death! . . . . (Act III, Sc. ii, *Plays,* II, pp. 435–436)

Passive submission even to the inevitable is not for a man of Kublai's stature. He will fight to the end for his own values and will persist in his attempt to make death meaningful. Since the force of reality must, as always, come into its own, the Kaan's dilemma is the eternal one that the very pride and dignity which save man can destroy him. He must acknowledge his humanity in both defiance and acceptance. When the nobles and priests have departed, Kublai turns to his friend Chu-yin, the sage.

KUBLAI: Oh, Chu-yin, my Wise Friend, was the prayer I taught them wisdom?

CHU-YIN: It was the wisdom of pride. It was thy wisdom.

· · · · · · · · · · · · · · · · · ·

KUBLAI: Was it not truth?

CHU-YIN: It was the truth of power. It was thy truth.

KUBLAI: My pride, my power? My wisdom, my truth? For me there remains only—her truth! . . . She died for the love of a fool!

CHU-YIN: No. She loved love. She died for beauty.

KUBLAI: Your words are hollow echoes of the brain. Do not wound me with wisdom. Speak to my heart! . . .

CHU-YIN: (*bowing—compassionately*) Then weep, old man. Be humble and weep for your child. . . . (Act III, Sc. ii, *Plays*, II, p. 437)

In tears the Kaan asserts his full humanity. No longer the exalted ruler, he is a grief-stricken grandfather, tested in his power to endure and embrace both pride and humility, defiance and acquiescence.

The conflicting opposites of *Marco Millions* wrestle, still, in *Desire Under the Elms* (1924), but now they take on a new identity. They are not only dream and reality, pride and love, exultation and pain. From *Desire* on, throughout the O'Neill canon, they are Father and Mother. Their over-whelming, unconscious influence upon the characters is expressed in terms roughly equivalent to the Oedipus and Electra complexes. A given character's proud, isolated, expansive self-image now resembles his father's face; the loving, sensitive, submissive self-image wears a mask of the mother. These parental opposites which gave the char-acter birth are at destructive war within him. Both de-mand expression; if he gives in entirely to his identification with one parent, action—and life—cease for him. The struggle is not limited to the mind of the hero. In fact, sometimes there is no hero. The maternal and paternal forces whose warfare is clearest in one character ultimately sway the destinies of all the characters. The parental im-ages are indifferent gods who plot the action of the drama as they wager and contend for human lives.

Desire Under the Elms is set on a farm in New England. The play is divided into three "parts," the first of which concerns the revolt of the Cabot brothers against their tyrannical father, Ephraim. Although the character of the youngest son, Eben, is the focal point of the play, Part I concentrates on the two elder brothers. They are clumsy, loutish sons of the soil, barely escaping the stock charac-terizations of stage Yankee and country bumpkin. Their dialogue and action give Part I a crudely comic flavor, suggesting a dramatic pattern which emerges fully in *The Iceman Cometh* and *Moon for the Misbegotten*. The play begins as comedy, but as O'Neill said with reference to *The Iceman Cometh,* it is not long before "the comedy breaks up and the tragedy comes on."

The father against whom the brothers are in rebellion is Ephraim Cabot, a self-centered, loveless man who has projected his own personality into that of his God, a tyrannic, ascetic, restrictive embodiment of Puritanism, "hard and lonesome and old" like Ephraim. He is a God whom Ephraim identifies with the farm itself, from the rocky soil of which he has by sheer doggedness won a living— "God's in the stones!" Ephraim, like the monomaniac "extremists," has dedicated his entire life to this God, who is, of course, only an image of his own ego. Ephraim has already sacrificed his sons by enslaving them to the farm, but the most pathetic sacrificial victim was his second wife (mother of Eben, the youngest son), a gentle, sensitive woman, whom he married not for love, but for land. She died overworked and love-starved, a victim of Ephraim's exploitive egotism.

Opposing the puritanical Ephraim and his God, in whose name love has been desecrated, is the spirit of this woman—her self-sacrifice, her longing for beauty, her need of natural sexual love which demands fulfillment. This second force is symbolized in the elms that tower over the farmhouse, dominating the entire play:

There is a sinister maternity in their aspect, a crushing, jealous absorption. . . . They brood oppressively over the house. They are like exhausted women resting their sagging breasts and hands and hair on its roof, and when it rains their tears trickle down monotonously and rot on the shingles. (Setting, *Plays*, I, p. 202)

The violated maternal spirit works its vengeance *

* The obvious classical precedents for this spirit of vengeful maternity appear in *Medea* and in the *Oresteia*. Mythologically, the Furies which pursue Orestes are female fertility symbols demanding retribution for his mother's murder.

through Eben, the son of the wronged woman, and through Abbie, the third wife, now Eben's stepmother. Abbie has married Ephraim for the same reason that he married Eben's mother, to acquire property. At first with separate selfish motives—Eben for revenge upon his father, and Abbie to have a son to inherit Ephraim's farm—the two determine to satisfy their desire for each other. Abbie, however, falls in love with Eben. Upon consummation of that love, the maternal ghost is somewhat placated—love has finally had natural sexual expression. After the event the room in which it took place, formerly that of Eben's mother, loses its oppressive, tomb-like atmosphere. As Abbie says,

> We made it our'n last night, didn't we? We give it life—our lovin' did. (*A pause.*)
> EBEN: (*with a strange look*) Maw's gone back t'her grave. She kin sleep now. (Part II, Sc. iv, *Plays*, I, p. 245)

But they have paid only a part of the ancestral debt. Their physical union has fulfilled the demand of the maternal ghost for normal sexuality, but Eben must still answer for his mother's thwarted spiritual needs. He is drawn to Abbie not by love, but by lust, greed, and the desire for revenge. Eben wears two figurative masks—one ruthless and self-centered like his father, the other sensitive and hungry for beauty and love as his mother was. O'Neill makes this double identity quite clear. While Eben constantly asserts that he is the "heir" of his mother—"I'm Maw—every drop o' blood!"—his brothers keep reminding him that he is the "spittin' image" of his father. His very determination to avenge his mother reflects the personality of his father; in buying out his brothers' share of the farm in order, eventually, to be sole owner, Eben demonstrates his father's greed; in desiring possession of his father's paramours (including a neighboring prostitute, as well as Abbie), he duplicates his father's lust. Eben must break down the mask of egotism, must cast off the prideful father, if he is to become integrated with his other self. The subsequent action of the play makes it possible for him to do so.

After a child is born to him and Abbie, Eben discovers her original motive in having the child, and threatens to leave her. To prove that her love is for Eben, not simply for the infant and his inheritance, Abbie kills the child. Furious at the act, Eben goes to the police to report her. In the process, however, he realizes that he, too, is guilty, that he must give himself up with Abbie, and accept with her the consequences of the crime. In the act of sacrificing himself, his vengeful lust is transformed into love. The two face death or imprisonment together, accepting with exultation the tragic irony that love has not come to fruition until the moment of inevitable loss, just as they accept without question the justice of their fate. In this acceptance they, like the other "finders," have found their integration. Unlike the couple of *The Straw,* there is no "hopeless hope" for them, nor do they seek it. In the reality of the situation itself they find salvation.

The opposing drives at war within Eben call to mind Horney's description of the strife within the pride system: the expansive and impossibly prideful image of the father is at war with the submissive, giving spirit of the mother. Even stated in terms of sexuality, of desire and its motives, the dichotomy is the same. Old Ephraim's Puritan conception of sex as an ugly, sinful necessity has perverted all sexuality into a brutal lust as egotistical and exploitive as his other greeds; but in the brooding maternal spirit symbolized by the elms sex is a spontaneous, beautiful, unselfish, and amoral life force, perverted into a powerful avenging spirit by suppression. O'Neill views this suppressed maternal aspect as Eben's "real" self, from which he has been alienated in his pursuit of the prideful father in himself. When Eben sacrifices his own life, with Abbie, he has relinquished the chase. The conflict is over, and he becomes capable of spontaneous love. In the young couple's fulfillment of their desire and in the transmutation of sex to love, reality has finally asserted itself, has struck through the illusory mask of pride.

But to "strike through the mask" is not to destroy it. For Pride remains in the person of the old man—although even he has shown some signs of the disunited self. He is locked so fast, however, inside the egotistical one that his only effort to reach beyond it is a failure. When the whole truth has been told about Abbie and Eben, Ephraim decides to escape the loneliness of the farm. He will go to California as his older sons have done, taking with him his hoarded savings. He discovers, however, first with fury, then with secret relief, that the money is gone, Eben having used it to buy out his brothers' shares of the farm. Laying the loss of the money to the will of God, Ephraim recognizes that he can never free himself from that tract of barren land nor does he want to. The farm *is* himself and his prison—like the cage of *The Hairy Ape* and the house of the Mannons in *Mourning Becomes Electra*—and only by staying there and working justice on himself can he find self-integration:

It's a-goin' to be lonesomer now than ever it war afore—an' I'm gittin' old, Lord-ripe on the bough. . . . (*Then stiffening*) Waal—what d'ye want? God's lonesome, hain't he? God's hard and lonesome! (Part III, Sc. iv, *Plays*, I, p. 268)

He, too, accepts the tragic fate and its justice.

The lovers find their integration in sacrifice; Ephraim finds his in its opposite, pride. Through the lovers, reality has found its paradoxical destructive-affirmative expression; in their death they have found life. Ephraim lives on, but within the eternal illusion which is living death— the illusion represented by the farm, the mask of his fatal pride. Circles of ironic significance widen around the final curtain speech, an innocuous comment dropped by the sheriff, in the presence of the lovers who "stand for a moment looking up raptly in attitudes strangely aloof and devout."

SHERIFF: (*looking around at the farm enviously—to his companion*) It's a jim-dandy farm, no denyin'. Wished I owned it! (Part III, Sc. iv, *Plays*, I, p. 269)

The psychic forces whose Olympian thunder rumbles beneath the elms in *Desire* rage into open war in *The Great God Brown* (1925). It is no accident that this play marks O'Neill's first use of masks on the stage to represent those warring forces, for *The Great God Brown* is an explicit if complex allegory of the "struggle to exist as masks among the masks of the living."

On a realistic level the struggle takes place in three people: Dion Anthony, the torn and tortured artist; his wife, Margaret; and his boyhood friend, later his employer and enemy, William (Billy) Brown. Allegorically, however, the characters are multiple and overlapping. They represent not only conflicting selves, but conflicting elements in modern society.

In a widely reprinted letter to the New York *Evening Post* of February 13, 1926, O'Neill explained to a puzzled public some of the meanings of the allegory. Any analysis of the play must rest in part, at least, on this letter.

The play begins with a prologue in which Dion and Billy, as boys, are both courting Margaret. Billy is a simple, outgoing, apparently "adjusted" boy who wears no mask. Dion, however, is already conscious of the strife between the "Dion" and "Anthony" in himself. His real face is "dark, spiritual, poetic, passionately supersensitive, helplessly unprotected in its childlike religious faith in life" (Prologue, *Plays*, III, p. 260), but the boy Dion wears a mask of Pan. Margaret falls in love with the mask, never even recognizing the other face beneath it. In O'Neill's words, Margaret is the "eternal girl-woman with a virtuous simplicity of instinct, properly oblivious to everything but the means to her end of maintaining the race."

Dion and Margaret are married, and the play proper opens seven years later. Dion's real face has changed to that of a withdrawn, suffering ascetic, while his Pan mask has become Satanic. O'Neill explains the character of Dion:

Dion Anthony—Dionysus and St. Anthony—the creative pagan acceptance of life, fighting eternal war with the masochistic life-denying spirit of Christianity as represented in St. Anthony —the whole struggle resulting in this modern day in mutual exhaustion—creative joy in life for life's sake frustrated, rendered abortive, distorted by morality from Pan into Satan, into a Mephistopheles mocking himself in order to feel alive; Christianity, once heroic in martyrs for its intense faith now pleading weakly for intense belief in anything, even Godhead itself.

While this is O'Neill's considered explanation of the philosophical allegory, Dion himself, when we first meet him in the Prologue, outlines the psychological allegory:

Why am I afraid to live, I who love life and the beauty of flesh and the living colors of earth and sky and sea? Why am I afraid of love, I who love love? Why am I afraid, I who am not afraid? Why must I pretend to scorn in order to pity? Why must I hide myself in self-contempt in order to understand? Why must I be so ashamed of my strength, so proud or my weakness? Why must I live in a cage like a criminal, defying and hating, I who love peace and friendship? . . . Why was I born without a skin, O God, that I must wear armor in order to touch or be touched?

More than paganism and Christianity are at war in Dion. This is a portrait of the central neurotic conflict within the pride system, where the real self which takes "creative joy in life for life's sake" is lost in the empty darkness between the submissive mask of St. Anthony and the aggressive mask of Mephistopheles. As the play progresses Dion can be his lost, bewildered, little-boy self only when his head is in the lap of Mother Earth—the archetypal image of the eternally protective mother to whom Dion longs to return.

In the play this mother is Cybel, who wears the mask of a prostitute, but is beneath it "an incarnation of Cybel, the Earth Mother doomed to segregation as a pariah in a world of unnatural laws but patronized by her segregators who are thus themselves the first victims of their laws."

The neurotic conflict in Dion makes him increasingly incapable of meeting the demands of outer reality. He is unable to paint, or to support his family in any way. Margaret, in desperation, goes to Brown, who offers Dion a job as designer in Brown's architectural firm. Dion accepts, but this enforced conformity only makes his condition worse. He longs to escape the conflict altogether in death. The first view of Dion in his capacity as designer finds him seated at a drafting table, reading aloud from the *Imitation of Christ*. His mask rests on the table before him. "Quickly must thou be gone from hence, see then how matters stand with thee. Ah, fool—learn now to die to the world that thou mayst begin to live with Christ. . . ." He picks up the Satanic mask and addresses it: "Peace, poor tortured one, brave pitiful pride of man, the hour of deliverance comes. Tomorrow we may be with Him in Paradise!"

Dion's expansive self, masked as Satan, is capable still of originality, but the inhibiting pressures of self-hatred and of society have distorted the spontaneous creative process into an artificial, grotesque parody of itself. He designs a cathedral which he describes to Brown:

And this cathedral is my masterpiece! It will make Brown the most eminent architect in this state of God's Country. I put a lot into it—what was left of my life! It's one vivid blasphemy from sidewalk to the tips of its spires!—but so concealed that the fools will never know. They'll kneel and worship the ironic Silenus who tells them the best good is never to be born! (Act II, Sc. iii, *Plays*, III, p. 297)

Dion's cathedral is a metaphor of the neurotic process—that terrifying paradox described by Horney—which O'Neill seems to have understood thoroughly throughout the play. Man's normal need to transcend himself, to build spires toward the infinite, is blasphemed and travestied when its energies are all diverted inward to the struggle with masks of self. The "poor pitiful pride of man" is only a "bad-boy" mask; it is not creative self-confidence but the sick compulsion to fight with and yield to the commands of shadows. Dion himself understands that he, as he is, is not really "man"—that is, a whole, fulfilled man. He is an artist who creates in spite of—not because of—his neurosis. He knows, however, that the sensitivity which cripples him and makes him suffer is also an unmistakable sign of life in him, and no such sign is apparent in William —The Great God—Brown.

Brown represents those forces in society which crush and at the same time exploit the talent of the artist. According to O'Neill, Brown is "the visionless demi-god of our new materialistic myth—a Success—building his life of exterior things, inwardly empty and resourceless, an uncreative creature of superficial preordained grooves, a by-product forced aside into slack waters by the main currents of life desire."

Brown is unmasked throughout the first half of the play. The self-image he follows is no problem to him—it was created for him by his father, to whose will Brown submitted without question. He is a conformist, who leads a comfortable existence, unaware of himself as an individual personality. Through Dion, however, Brown grows toward self-awareness. His growth begins with his knowledge and envy of the latent power in Dion. Apparently the loser in the eyes of society, Dion possesses what Brown most covets—love (in Margaret and the children) and creative talent. And Brown, of course, understands neither. He does not recognize the unhappiness of Dion's marriage any more than he does the satire of Dion's designs.

Brown is soon to have his desire, however; he will be like Dion and pay the price. Dion successfully destroys himself, and, dying, leaves to Brown the Satanic mask of pride which falls off as Dion weakens at Brown's feet. The martyred face of the submissive Dion begs forgiveness of Brown, asking "What was the prayer, Billy? I'm getting so sleepy. . . ."

BILLY: (*in a trancelike tone*) "Our Father who art in Heaven."
DION: (*drowsily*) "Our Father" . . . (Act II, Sc. iii, *Plays,* III, p. 299)

O'Neill called this scene a parable of modern Christianity's begging for a faith in Godhead at the feet of materialism:

It is as Mephistopheles he [Dion] falls stricken at Brown's feet after having condemned Brown to destruction by willing him his mask, but, this mask falling off as he dies, it is the Saint who kisses Brown's feet in abject contrition and pleads as a little boy to a big brother to tell him a prayer.

Brown puts on the mask of Dion, and tries to become him, but the mask destroys Brown as it did Dion.

Brown has always envied the creative life force in Dion—what he himself lacks. When he steals Dion's mask of Mephistopheles he thinks he is gaining the power to live creatively while in reality he is only stealing that creative power made self-destructive by complete frustration. This devil of mocking doubt makes short work of him. It enters him, rending him apart, torturing and transfiguring him until he is even forced to wear a mask of his success, William A. Brown, before the world, as well as Dion's mask toward wife and children. And thus he partakes of Dion's anguish—more poignantly, for Dion had the Mother, Cybel—and in the end out of this anguish his soul is born, a tortured Christian soul such as the dying Dion's, begging for belief, and at last finding it on the lips of Cybel.

When Brown assumes Dion's identity he is beset not only with the inner struggle, but with the practical necessity of concealing the death of the real Dion, whose body Brown has buried in his garden. As the force of Dion's mask works upon him, Brown becomes sensitive and consciously alive, but this only intensifies his frustration and guilt. Unable to bear the strain of concealment and of double identity longer, he attempts to kill the Billy Brown in himself and to find integration as one person, as Dion. Discarding the mask of Brown, he attempts, as Dion did, to escape by returning to the Mother, Cybel. But the mask of Brown which he left behind in his office looks to society like the body of Billy Brown. Dion (Brown) is accused of murder, is followed by the police, and shot. This final ironic twist is a statement of his dilemma—that he cannot kill the Billy Brown in himself without killing also its opposite, the Dion Anthony, for as Cybel recognizes, he is now Dion Brown. His name is also, as Cybel tells the police, Man.

In Brown's dying prayer at the end O'Neill shouts his affirmation of the tragic spirit—almost literally as it ap-

pears in the origins of tragedy in ritual celebrating the
death of the fertility god, Dionysus. Here as there the god
dies and is reborn in one rite. Flowing between the inevitable opposites of pride and humility, joy and sorrow,
birth and death, life takes meaning from process.

BROWN: . . . I don't want justice. I want love.

CYBEL: There is only love.

BROWN: Thank you, Mother. (*Then feebly*) I'm getting sleepy.
What's the prayer you taught me?—Our Father—?

CYBEL: (*with calm exultance*) Our Father Who Art!

BROWN: (*taking her tone—exultantly*) Who art! Who art!
(*Suddenly with ecstasy*) I know! I have found Him! I hear
Him speak! "Blessed are they that weep, for they shall laugh!"
Only he that has wept can laugh! . . .

CYBEL: . . . Always spring comes again bearing life! Always
again!   Always, always, forever again!—Spring again!—life
again!—summer, and fall and death and peace again!—(*With
agonized sorrow*)—but always, always, love and conception
and birth and pain again—spring bearing the intolerable
chalice of life again—(*Then with agonized exultance*)—
bearing the glorious, blazing crown of life again! (*She stands
like an idol of Earth, her eyes staring out over the world.*)
(Act IV, Sc. ii, *Plays*, III, pp. 322–323)

For all this ecstatic affirmation, with its embarrassing
pseudo-poetry, the lines that stick in the reader's mind
are those bitterly prosaic ones of Dion Brown's as he pre-
pares to seek annihilation: "This is Daddy's bedtime secret
for today: Man is born broken. He lives by mending. The
grace of God is glue!" (Act IV, Sc. i, *Plays*, III, p. 318)

In his description of the "broken" elements of man and
of the mending process O'Neill drew heavily upon the

ideas and symbols of Jungian psychology. Among these are Jung's version of the Oedipus pattern, and his principles of the "shadow" and the "persona," of "inevitable complementariness," and "individuation." Following the Oedipus configuration Dion longs to return to an archetypal mother who is the warm, protective spirit of "all-being." He flees to her for refuge from the restrictive, but at the same time driving, force of the father in himself. The further splitting of Dion between the martyr and the Mephistopheles, with his gradual absorption into the latter, reflects Jung's concept of the "shadow." This is the evil *Doppelgänger* who follows us all, "the inferior and less commendable part of a person." [1] With growing disappointment, conflict, and despondency, the shadow may assimilate the ego, and if it does so, then the outward personality shows a "change for the worse in character," while "the ego becomes more infantile and primitive as a result of the assimilation; the man becomes boyish." [2]

All the characters of *The Great God Brown* wear, at one time or another, the mask Jung calls the "persona." Under normal conditions the *persona* serves as an "elastic barrier" between the individual and society, which permits him to communicate more easily with his fellows. The danger of the *persona*, however, is that under stress and through habit it loses its elasticity; "it stiffens, becomes automatic, and in the real meaning of the word, a grown-on mask, behind which the individual shrivels and runs the risk of becoming ever more empty." [3]

The mending process through which both Dion and Brown must pass in order to become integrated "man" constitutes an acceptance and absorption into the self of what Jung calls "inevitable complementariness." Brown recognizes this principle in his dying insight, "Only he that has wept can laugh!" When Cybel interprets this duality of joy and sorrow as part of the natural process of growth through opposites—"always love and conception and birth and pain again," she unites, as Jung does, the idea of "inevitable complementariness" with that of what Jung calls "individuation." Through this process, the whole, realized individual self emerges from the deep-lying "river" of life whose undulating flow results from the interaction of irreconcilable opposites. Individuation takes place only when the opposites of self—both the Dion and the Brown—can be combined in the individual in a sort of harmonious compromise, when the tension between opposites is not resolved, but accepted as the inevitable condition of all growth and change.

Obviously, Jung's is not the only voice heard in *The Great God Brown*. Rising above it, perhaps, in Cybel's final paean, is that of Nietzsche. The entire Christ-Dionysus dichotomy is, of course, Nietzschean. And the Dionysus whose death and resurrection are symbolized in "the pagan acceptance of life"—acceptance of Nietzsche's "eternal recurrence" and "transvaluation of former values" —is the Dionysus of *The Birth of Tragedy*. He is also the hero of *Lazarus Laughed* (1925-27), where he embraces destiny with the rhapsodic, almost hysterical, affirmation of Zarathustra.

Lazarus is the last and most vehement of the "finders"; he has made his discovery at the beginning of the play, when he appears as a joyful and integrated character, the only one who does not wear a mask. He has returned from death, resurrected by Jesus, in whose eyes he found the secret which he knows is man's salvation. His mission is to preach the doctrine of his discovery to mankind. The play is a vast symbolic pageant, tracing the progress of Lazarus as he preaches to the Jews, the Greeks, and finally, the Romans. In Rome he meets the resistance of Caligula and Tiberius, who represent the primary inhibiting forces which Lazarus must fight—pride with its accompanying fear of loneliness; the false desire for life which is actually a whimpering fear of death. Lazarus is finally burned at the stake, still affirming with his magnificent laughter his secret—"There is no death!"

What Lazarus has learned is that death is only a stage of natural process, one step in the continuum of perpetual "becoming" which is existence. The conception of death as finality is a mistake; the conception of it as evil is equally mistaken. Death is no more good or evil than its opposites, life and birth. It is man who projects death's evil significance upon it and then fears it—fears, in a sense, his own creation. This is the insight Lazarus has gained beyond the grave—that death is man's invention and can exist only by virtue of man's persistent fear of it. The fear of death and of loneliness are the whips with which man flagellates himself and which tyrants—here, Caligula and Tiberius—use to destroy man's will.

If fear of death is a projection of man's needs and values, then the cure for it lies within man. He can and must embrace his destiny with the positive love which is only the inevitable opposite of that negative hate which produces fear. The message Lazarus brings from Jesus is, "There is Eternal Life in No . . . and there is the same Eternal Life in Yes! Death is the fear beween!" (Act I, Sc. i, *Plays*, I, p. 279) The hope for man is in love, "love for his life on earth, a noble love above suspicion and distrust! . . .

Man has always suspected his life, and in revenge and self-torture his love has been faithless!" (Act IV, Sc. i, *Plays*, I, p. 461) And one cannot love life without loving death also, since they are phases of the same cycle, and are significant only in relation to each other.

In referring to death as eternal life, O'Neill does not mean the eternal life of the individual will or conscious ego. It is the individual will—the self—which limits us, and which makes us proud and fearful of the loneliness and loss of that will which is death. As always in O'Neill's work, the conscious ego in its effort to control the unconscious, to preserve its proud individual will, limits and divides the personality. In Jungian terms it is as if the individual ego emerges for a while from the vast realm of the personal and collective unconscious, fights to maintain itself against the encroachments and control of the unconscious, and finally, when the tension is relaxed, sinks back into the unconscious, only to emerge again, continually repeating the process, but in different individuals. This is not a concept of reincarnation of an individual soul but, as Jung points out, is comparable to the organic conception of the conservation of energy—here, psychic rather than physical energy. No matter what we may think of the truth or falsity of this concept, there is little doubt that O'Neill actually had it in mind while working on *Lazarus Laughed,* since at the same time (spring of 1926) he was beginning work on *Strange Interlude,* where the tension between the conscious and the unconscious and the pattern of emergence and regression become explicit.*

* A further link between the two plays is the influence of Schopenhauer. *Lazarus Laughed* echoes many of the concepts and even some of the wording of the chapter entitled, "On Death and Its Relation to the In-

Lazarus has tapped the underground sea from which "the fountain" of process springs and to which it ultimately returns. The living motion of that sea is in the ebb and flow of individual consciousness at strife with unconscious being—the father and mother of life and the self. His discovery encompasses that made by all the other finders who learn that the only unity is to be found in disunity. Man moves and grows only as long as the tension between the opposites exists. His hopeless effort to reconcile them demands from him the action and creativity which lead to self-realization. For the finders, to be torn between masks of self, to be unable to accept relative values, is to be alive. Integration or the discovery of an absolute other than change and process is death.

By accepting the disunity of process, the finders have rediscovered their lost harmony with nature. Man's inner life moves through the cycle of birth and death as nature moves. The unity of his life is organic, infused with one creative spirit within which all opposites are one. The link between the organic continuum of nature and the life of the individual man—the bridge from analogy to unity—is to be found within the unconscious mind of the man himself. Here the evidence of his oneness with nature and with other men is displayed in universal symbols. Through their analogies to natural phenomena and to common experience he sees all men and nature in himself. Such evidence, of course, has the status of proof only if one is

---

destructibility of our True Nature," from *The World as Will and Idea. Strange Interlude*, also, as Doris Alexander has pointed out in "*Strange Interlude* and Schopenhauer" (*American Literature*, XXV [May, 1953], pp. 213–228), reflects Schopenhauer's philosophy, particularly the idea of the subjection of individual existence to the blind force of the Will to Live.

willing to make a mystical leap into truth by way of intuition. Ultimately, this is a leap to faith made by the finders after a lifelong search.

It is by no means, however, a comfortable faith, but rather a faith in pain itself. The finders cannot settle for the extremist's mad fulfillment of the ego, or for the searcher's bewilderment, evasion, or escape "beyond the horizon." Some of them, Michael, Jim, Eben, do find the answer in self-sacrifice, but only after a long, conscious battle with the ego. They are well aware that pride is their sin, but this awareness comes into direct conflict with their knowledge that this same pride is indispensable to them—that without their individuality and self-respect they would become, as Jim finally does, mere passive shadows of the object of their sacrifice. They must accept both the pride and humility of being man, artist, or lover, with faith in the dependence of life upon the tragic fact that there can never be perfection, nor even a perfect balance between the opposites, but there must always be a tension which pulls us toward one, only to pull back toward the other. This is the torment which man is driven to celebrate in all his symbol-making arts—but most literally and specifically in tragedy. O'Neill explained his philosophy of tragic drama, as well as of tragic life, in an interview in 1922:

I suppose it is the idea I try to put into all of my plays. People talk of the "tragedy" in them, and call it "sordid," "depressing," "pessimistic"—the words usually applied to anything of a tragic nature. But tragedy, I think, has the meaning the Greeks gave it. To them it brought exaltation, an urge toward life and ever more life. It roused them to deeper spiritual understandings

and released them from the petty greeds of everyday existence. When they saw a tragedy on the stage they felt their
own hopeless hopes ennobled into art. . . . Any victory we
may win is never the one we dreamed of winning. The point
is that life in itself is nothing. It is the dream that keeps us
fighting, willing—living! [4]

Lazarus Laughed is an attempt to illustrate this definition of tragedy. As in *The Great God Brown,* the central
allegory alludes to the Dionysian rites. Obviously, in his
use of the Hebraic Lazarus who gains a Greek insight
from Christ, O'Neill implies analogy between the Christian, Hebraic, and Greek mythological patterns. His real
emphasis, however, is upon the ritual death of Lazarus as
Dionysus—"Not," says O'Neill,

the coarse, drunken Dionysus, nor the effeminate God, but
Dionysus in his middle period, more comprehensive in his symbolism, the soul of the recurring seasons, of living and dying
as processes in eternal growth, of the wine of life stirring forever in the sap and blood and loam of things. (Act II, Sc. i,
Plays, I, p. 415)

But ritual is one thing and drama another. By his delib-
erate use of established symbols O'Neill has conceptualized his philosophy in *Lazarus Laughed,* but he has not
dramatized it. He has become what Emerson called not
a poet (or creative artist), but a mystic who attempts to
"nail a meaning" to a given symbol. If drama is an imitation of life—a transmogrification of experience—its philosophy should be an underlying assumption. To emerge from
myth and ritual, drama should "act out" man's dilemma,
not explain it in intellectual and expository terms. The

artist who truly affirms existence does not need to thunder his affirmation like a baritone at a musicale, singing "I love life!" His work is itself an affirmation—even if it is only an affirmation, like Kafka's, of man's power to protest his helplessness. O'Neill does not convince us, because he protests too much.

Far more than an artistic flaw in *Lazarus Laughed* is suggested here. The dependence upon allegorical symbols and upon explication rather than implication to give the drama life and meaning produces only a synthetic imitation of a fully developed art form—here of tragedy. The resulting structure is Dion's cathedral where the mask of Dionysus only disguises the sneer of a grinning Silenus.

Similarly, the discovery of Lazarus and the finders, while valid enough in its philosophical outlines, does not represent a true psychological solution to the problem of disintegration. It, too, is an imitation, a rationalized description of the process of self-realization which, if genuine, is felt and acted without the necessity of exposition or artificially imposed symbols. O'Neill was writing in these plays not about what the finders discovered, but about what they—and he—longed desperately to find.

This period (1921–31) was O'Neill's most creative one. He never ceased working until he became afflicted with Parkinson's disease, about 1943—but the steady stream of finished work slowed almost to a halt while he struggled with drafts of *Days Without End* between 1931 and 1934. No doubt there were many explanations for this sudden drying of the springs which will be made clear in biography, but the basic cause is implied in the meaning of true self-realization, as opposed to the quality of the "unity" which the finders discovered in disunity.

What Horney calls self-realization has its counterpart in the Jungian concept of individuation. Jung's definition of this process in *Two Essays in Analytical Psychology* might have been written by Horney:

Individuation means to become a single, discrete being, and inasmuch as the concept of individuality embraces that innermost, last, and incomparable uniqueness of our being, it also includes the idea of becoming one's own real self. Hence, individuation could also be translated as "coming into selfhood," or "self-realization." [5]

The road to the discovery of the real self must lead first to a tearing down of the illusions about the self. This "destructive" therapy is aimed at the pride system, that conflict between the expansive and the self-effacing images of the self which have been set up to comply with the "tyrannic shoulds." Only when the neurotic has seen this conflict for what it is, can he resolve it and discover his "real self" which awaits development. Only when he can forget the "great man" that he should be and the humble, submissive man that he also should be, can he discover the real man that he is. Then only, according to Horney, can he know what he really wants and feels, not what pride motivates him to want and feel:

He will develop then the unique alive forces of his real self: the clarity and depth of his own feelings, thoughts, wishes, interests; the ability to tap his own resources, the strength of his own will power; the special capacities or gifts he may have; the faculty to express himself, and to relate himself to others with his spontaneous feelings. [6]

The way to this goal is difficult and fraught with all the dangers of any voyage in self-discovery, for the defenses of the pride system are formidable—often the result of years of careful, self-protective building—and can be broken down only with long and careful treatment. The man who emerges successfully, however, has come to accept himself as he *is*, with all the imperfections he may have as a human being. He may be aware of diverse self-images; he may affirm the relativity of value in a world of opposite values, and accept it as an indispensable accompaniment of life. Nevertheless, he will be capable of formulating his own values and acting according to them. On his way to self-realization he will have seen and recognized the pull between the opposites of the pride system; and when they have been de-valued by appearing as the illusions that they are, he may still recognize opposites within himself, but the healthy man will make a consistent choice as to which image is really himself, and will act on that choice as an integrated person.

When we examine what O'Neill seems to be doing in the light of Horney's theory, we see that the real disunity which he is affirming is that of the neurotic conflict itself— the battle between the expansive and self-effacing drives which takes place within the pride system. In these plays the characters find only a new pseudosolution; they do not discover the real self beneath the conflicting masks; they only discover the masks, which they mistakenly think constitute the totality of self. The analogy the finders see between the opposite self-images and the opposites of nature, and their belief that they have discovered in the tides of the unconscious the same absorptive, reconciling power that ebbs and flows through the life process—this "discovery" only sharpens the poignancy of their delusion. Objectively "true" or not, the analogy is actually a rationalization (in all senses of the word) of the character's dilemma and offers him, too late, a promise of escape. He has not solved the problem of conflict; he has only found a kind of justification for a life wasted in the attempt to solve it.

We think of Juan in his lifelong effort to decide whether he is a conqueror or a poet—finally effacing the whole problem by his absorption and forgetfulness in the fountain; Jim in *All God's Chillun*, finding himself by losing himself in his self-image as a grovelling black slave; Marco Polo, drowning the poet in himself in the masterful imperialist, while Kukachin effaces herself in Tao; old "hard and lonesome" Ephraim finding his aggressive "solution" in identification with the farm, while Eben finds his Lethe in sacrifice. In *The Great God Brown* all the battles are fought within the pride system. The sacrificial "should" of asceticism perverts the masterful "should" of paganism; the "should" of financial success warps the "should" of creativity. The only escape is in the lap of Mother Earth, where Dion finally lays his head, then raises it briefly to exult in his discovery, before he dies. Margaret lives on in her illusion, but Dion has died in his. Even in *Welded*, the relationship follows perfectly the pattern described by Horney as "morbid dependency." In their utter dependence on each other and their simultaneous need to dominate each other, the couple move completely at the mercy of the demons of the pride system—never really escaping the "auras of egoism." Finally, in counterpoint to that wild rhapsody in which Lazarus roars his unity with himself and life, we hear the tormented cry of Nietzsche, falling in disintegration between his dream of the Superman and his bad conscience—the expansive Dionysus and the submissive Christ in himself—and signing his last, incoherent notes, *The Crucified.*

The pride system in which O'Neill's finders struggle is the offspring of unconscious self-hatred and indisputable evidence of it. To plunge more deeply into final explanations, to determine the ultimate source of the self-hatred, is in the realm not of criticism, but of professional psychoanalysis. For our purposes it is enough to observe and trace the persistent pattern of self-hatred in O'Neill's plays, and to guess that this was the pattern it took in his own mind. O'Neill rejected himself in all his characterizations of idealists, dreamers, artists—those poor devils whose self-images have arisen as the progeny of irreconcilable "tyrannic shoulds." They must be sensitive and creative, but they must also be economically and socially successful. They must be absorbed in a great love, but they must be emotionally free and independent. In effort and agony each wastes his life doing and being what he "should"—never knowing what he *wants* to do and be, or what he is. O'Neill sought with his characters the solution to the conflict, and his discovery, like that of the finders, was an intellectualization of a philosophy which to be real must be felt and, once felt, no longer requires conscious formulation in allegorical symbols.

Francis Fergusson puts his finger on the relationship of O'Neill's self-hatred to the plays:

O'Neill's plays are crosses. Follow the road he travels and you will often hear the sound of flagellation. Look and you will see that the whip is brought down by a tormented soul on his own back. But flowers grow on this desert track, and the mountains and the sunset lie *Beyond the Horizon*. The very imperfection which connects the author with his play also connects the author with his audience. . . . He offers us the act of seeking, but no disinterested contemplation; himself, therefore, rather than his work. Only the dead cease to change; but by discipline it is sometimes possible to produce a work complete and independent of the suffering individual. O'Neill's failings may be ascribed to the fact that he has never found any such discipline.[7]

It is this discipline of objectivity that O'Neill or any artist requires in order to convert experience into art through symbols—but the very nature of O'Neill's own experience, the self he gives the audience in his work, is such that he *cannot* transcend it into objectivity.

O'Neill lived according to his own "Dogma for the New Masked Drama," wherein "One's outer life passes in a solitude haunted by the masks of others; one's inner life passes in a solitude hounded by the masks of oneself." [8] The tragic tension between opposite masks does result in a kind of creativity and action, to be sure, but it is not directed toward the objective world which demands such action. It is directed within and against the self. In this sense the tension is not really a supporting framework, a psychological and moral order within which one can move and produce. It is a trap from which there is no escape, where one is doomed to lifelong participation in a conflict between values and self-conceptions.

Paradoxically, O'Neill's work becomes more powerful and substantial, more "independent of the suffering individual," when it deals with the conflict from this point of view—when he treats life as a more truly dramatic tragedy, wherein the affirmation is implicit in the dignity of the struggle and the struggle is frankly a neurotic one. *Strange Interlude, Dynamo,* and *Mourning Becomes Electra* are honest attempts to interpret the classic universals of character in the terms of neurosis. O'Neill meets squarely the pathological nature of the struggle with masks: a tragic waste of human life, a pitiful destruction of the real and growing self by the pride system, whose ignorant armies clash by night.

The pride which traps the protagonists of *Strange Interlude* (1927), *Dynamo* (1928), and *Mourning Becomes Electra* (1931), wears, of course, the mask of the father. The characters long to escape him and to find their mother, the Cybel of love and free acceptance, but she is theirs only briefly, if at all, and father claims them for his own at last. To the embattled ego, father is now the expansive, self-centered, and isolated image of itself; he is also the rigid puritanical force—the superego—which forbids his child to give expression to the drives of the id—the libido, the mother. This ideal mother for whom all men long still exists in human consciousness, still represents peace, freedom, and spontaneous love. But embodied in real women, in an actual mother, she reflects not Cybel, but Cybel dominated by the father-image in herself. For her children, however, there is no unity in their disunity; mother cannot kiss them and make them well as she does the finders. Her kiss, like father's, can be a kiss of death.

Nina Leeds, heroine of *Strange Interlude,* is one of these father-dominated mothers. Poetically as well as literally, life begins for her with her father, in whose gigantic shadow the entire play is acted. From him she inherits the passionatey selfish hunger for love which determines her fate. His egotism sets the play in motion when, because of his desire to keep Nina near him, Professor Leeds has persuaded her aviator lover not to marry Nina until he returns from the war. The lover, Gordon, is killed, and Nina is left with agonizing regret and a sense of guilt that she did not insist upon marriage or did not at least give herself to him before he left.

Professor Leeds is a scholar—withdrawn, isolated, and ascetic—but "Puritanism" as such is not, as some critics have said,[1] his real motive or the primary force opposing Nina. His attitude may indicate what Richard Dana Skinner calls a "denial and prevention of creation," [2] but Leeds himself unequivocally reveals the true spring of his action and the motif of the play. He does so when he admits that it was he who prevented Nina's union with her lover, but defends himself by saying that he did it "for her sake":

NINA: . . . It's too late for lies.
PROFESSOR LEEDS: (*woodenly*) Let us say then that I *persuaded* myself it was for your sake. That may be true. You are

young. You think one can live with truth. Very well. It is
also true that I was jealous of Gordon. I was alone and
wanted to keep your love. I hated him as one hates a thief
one may not accuse nor punish. I did my best to prevent
your marriage. I was glad when he died. There. Is that what
you wish me to say?

NINA: Yes. Now I begin to forget I've hated you. You were
braver than I, at least. (Act I, *Plays*, I, p. 20)

After the death of the lover, Nina attempts to assuage
her guilt toward him by "sacrificing" her body to wounded
war veterans, but she has already missed her one real
opportunity for sacrifice. It was inevitable that she should,
for her destiny is this very selfishness. She dedicates her
life to the struggle against her fate, but each attempt only
tightens the coils around her. The promiscuity which she
thought of as "giving" turns out to have been a sordid,
masochistic attempt at oblivion and brings only further
guilt and self-hatred. Nina begs Charlie Marsden, an old
family friend and her substitute "father" (Leeds having
died), to punish her, explaining that she intended kindness
to the men, "But it's horribly hard to give anything, and
frightful to receive! And to give love—oneself—not in this
world!" (Acts II, *Plays*, I, p. 45)

Gordon was Nina's one hope of release. He was a symbol
of love—of the escape from the prideful mask of the father
—a sort of redeeming trinity representing the ideal husband, lover, and son. After Gordon's death, this trinity is
unattainable in one man, but Nina hopes to find it in three
men—Sam, her husband, Ned, her lover, by whom she has
her son, and that son, Gordon, the third member of the
trinity. Each of these represents an opportunity for Nina

to love, but the inexorable power of the father-image turns each love into destructive possessiveness and exploitation.

After her father's death, his voice, speaking through Marsden, advises Nina to marry Sam Evans although she does not love him, in order to shape his career and to have children—with the reasoning that "when children come, love comes, you know." (Act II, *Plays*, I, p. 46) The tragic reversal—*peripateia*—occurs when Nina discovers that, unknown to Sam, his family has a long history of hereditary insanity, and Nina should not bear his child. But for Sam's sake as well as her own, she feels she must have a child, and she asks Ned Darrell, a young doctor, to be the father.

Before their son is born, however, Darrell and Nina have fallen in love. Passionately possessive, Nina wants her lover and child all to herself. She plans to desert Sam, even though she knows that such an act would kill him. Ned refuses to be a party to that crime and leaves on a long journey, not to return for years.

The son, Gordon, is born and Nina turns to him to fill her need to love, but still she is capable only of exploitation. She dominates Gordon's childhood, and when as a young man he is engaged to marry she repeats her father's behavior by attempting to prevent the marriage. Darrell returns, to discover that he no longer loves Nina and is free again to realize his own potentialities and to see Nina objectively. He warns Nina: "You've got to give up owning people, meddling in their lives as if you were God and had created them!" When Darrell later foils her attempt to prevent Gordon's marriage, Nina has lost all her men. Sam has died, the affair with Ned is over, and the second Gordon has flown away. Nina is too old and tired now to

batter any longer the walls of self in order to find love beyond them. The tragic pull between her need to give and
her need to take is over; now she can slip back into the
comfortable arms of her own ego, that father-mother per-
sonified in Charlie Marsden.

For when Darrell accuses Nina of playing God, he is
reflecting a basic change in O'Neill's conception of the
archetypal Woman. Throughout the play Nina has re-
belled against the idea of God the Father, "whose chest
thunders with egotism and is too hard for tired heads and
thoroughly comfortless." On the contrary, she says,

We should have imagined life as created in the birth-pain of
God the Mother. Then we would understand why we, Her children, have inherited pain, for we would know that our life's
rhythm beats from Her great heart, torn with the agony of love
and birth. And we would feel that death meant reunion with
Her, a passing back into her substance, blood of Her blood
again, peace of Her peace! (Act II, *Plays*, I, pp. 42–43)

Nina becomes herself an embodiment of God the Mother,
but she is not the Cybel she describes here, angel of be-
neficence and peace. She thunders her own brand of egotism inherited from her father. In her the eternal feminine
no longer redeems man but devours him, and his attempts
to free himself only damn him further to endless guilt and
self-hatred. This is the position of Woman from now on in
O'Neill's work. Yet, like all his "villains," male or female,
she is an object of compassion, herself longing for a mother,
for peace, for love, for innocence. To find them she must
become a child again, as Nina does when she falls asleep
in Charlie's arms at the end of the play.

When the struggle ceases for Nina, it is over also for the other characters, whose conflicts are parallel to hers. All of them live in a world of masks of the self and others. In place of the device of stage masks to show conflicting selves, O'Neill has substituted the use of dialogue and soliloquy. In soliloquies the hidden motives and conflicts of the inner self are revealed, in contrast to the outward *persona* shown to others in the dialogue. Some of the masks are those of familiar faces. Sam Evans is another Billy Brown. Ned is another sensitive intellectual who fights the love which saps and absorbs his creative power, only to discover finally that love itself has been killed in the struggle. And Marsden is the boy-man who lives his life in his mother's lap. In the play he has been possessed by his mother as Nina was by her father and is so identified with his mother that he has become as much feminine as masculine.

When Nina turns to Charlie, at last the life-giving and life-destroying tension between the father- and mother-images dissolves. Nina has always seen life as "a strange dark interlude in the electrical displays of God the father." Now the lightning has ceased, its opposite charges neutralized in Charlie's sexlessness.

The lightning flashes again through *Dynamo*, where it pursues the hero—named, significantly, Reuben Light—to madness and death. Reuben's father is a fundamentalist minister, preaching the gospel of an angry God who speaks to him through the lightning, of which he has a pathological fear. Reuben, too, dreads the lightning. It represents for him the merciless tyranny not only of God the Father, but of his own father.

At the beginning of the play Reuben is caught in a feud between his father and an atheist, Ramsay Fife, whose daughter Reuben loves. Using this love as a weapon against the minister, Fife involves Reuben in a scheme which ultimately makes Reuben appear to be a coward and his father a fool. Reuben confides in his mother who, jealous of his love for Ada Fife, betrays him to his father.

Tormented by his mother's possessiveness and duplicity and by his father's fury, Reuben leaves home renouncing his parents and the God in whose name they have justified their behavior. Ada, too, has been false to him by taking part in her father's scheme. Reuben rejects her and romantic love, seeing her now as an object only of physical desire.

Thus Reuben's new materialistic attitude along with the Puritan restrictions of his heritage have turned love to lust. This is in contrast to the simple, amoral sexuality represented by the Cybel figure of this play, May Fife, Ada's mother. With her own unthinking faith in the cycle of love, marriage, and birth, she tries to reconcile the lovers, but Reuben, of course, is cut off by his own drives from this world of freedom which May represents.

He turns all the force of his frustrated need of God and love into a worship of electricity. In his fascination with his new god, he loses his fear of lightning—of the old God. But he is not destined to remain long in this state of atheistic security. It collapses completely when he goes home to discover that his mother has died, pleading for her son's return and forgiveness. Insane with guilt and grief, he concentrates his now fanatical faith in electricity in worship of the actual dynamo in the hydroelectric plant where he works. To Reuben the dynamo is God and

Mother. In its name he vows asceticism; his passion for
Ada becomes a sin which he must obliterate. In a final
mad scene on the ladder leading to a platform around the
dynamo, he shoots and kills Ada who, as Sin, prevents him
from union with his God, and, as another woman, prevents
him from union with his mother. Then he casts himself
to his death by electrocution against the dynamo, crying:

> I don't want any miracle, Mother! I don't want to know the
> truth! I only want you to hide me, Mother! Never let me go
> from you again! Please, Mother! (Act III, Sc. iii, *Plays*, III,
> p. 488)

Reuben has found his final integration. The dynamo—
that irresistible materialism which draws him to his destruction—is the mother whom he loved and by whom he
was betrayed, but it was God the Father's lightning, flowing through the dynamo, that killed him.

In a much quoted and important letter to George Jean
Nathan, O'Neill outlined his intention in writing *Dynamo:*

> [The play] is a symbolical and factual biography of what
> is happening in a large section of the American (and not only
> American) soul right now. It is really the first play of a trilogy
> that will dig at the roots of the sickness of today as I feel it—
> the death of the old God and failure of science and material-
> ism to give any satisfactory new one for the surviving primi-
> tive religious instinct to find a meaning for life in, and to
> comfort its fears of death with. It seems to me that anyone
> trying to do big work nowadays must have this big subject
> behind all the little subjects of his plays or novels, or he is
> scribbling around the surface of things, and has no more real
> status than a parlor entertainer. . . .[3]

O'Neill has obviously used the Oedipus pattern in order to give the symbolic conflict a basis in "factual biography," but the conflict is so overt and intense that the play becomes a nightmare of insanity, rather than a convincing allegory of modern man's dilemma. The factual or clinical overwhelms the symbolic, and Reuben is not a universal or representative figure, but only a poor lunatic at the mercy of his unconscious drives. While the characters of *Strange Interlude* and *Mourning Becomes Electra* are neurotic, doomed to move within the limits of the pride system, still they move with dignity and sanity, submitting only after a heroic struggle. Reuben is a puppet, whose agony is only the jerking of the strings.

In *Mourning Becomes Electra*, O'Neill leaves for a while the war between God and science and returns to the more limited conflict within the "suffering individual." But the conflict and the suffering are traceable more specifically than ever to the fixations upon father and mother, to the tension between Puritanism and freedom, pride and love, death and life. As before, in most of the plays since *Desire Under the Elms* all other masks and values stem from the power of the father- and mother-images, the Oedipus and Electra complexes. In his detailed "Working Notes and Extracts from a Fragmentary Work Diary," O'Neill outlines his purpose and method in *Mourning Becomes Electra*, emphasizing repeatedly his equation of the complexes with destiny. They are "a modern tragic interpretation of classic fate without benefit of Gods—for it [the play] must, before everything, remain [a] modern psychological play—fate springing out of the family." [4]

As with the original Atreidae, the family fate of the

New England Mannons is ancestral, not limited to one generation. It has been set in motion before the opening of the play by Abe Mannon, father of Ezra (Agamemnon) and grandfather of Lavinia and Orin (Electra and Orestes). Abe's younger brother, David, had been involved in a liaison with a French-Canadian governess, Marie Brantôme, resulting in her pregnancy. David married her, but Abe (in Lavinia's words) "put them both out of the house and then afterwards tore it down and built this one because he wouldn't live where his brother had disgraced the family." The child of David and Marie is Adam Brant, the Aegisthus of the play, who returns to avenge his parents' death in poverty and misery after their exile.

The house of Mannon, therefore, was built upon outraged pride and Puritanism, leading inevitably to death for the Mannon line. For them pride is the source of death, and love is the source of life. Existence for the Mannons is a life-in-death from which love, represented by Marie Brantôme, has been shut out. This living death is reflected in the faces of the family, "life-like death masks," and in their home, a sepulcher, "the 'whited' one of the Bible—pagan temple front stuck like a mask on Puritan gray ugliness." ("Homecoming," Act I, *Plays*, II, p. 17) O'Neill clarifies this idea in his "Notes": "What I want from this mask concept is a dramatic arresting visual symbol of the separateness, the fated isolation of this family. . . . [The] Mannon drama takes place on a plane where outer reality is a mask of true fated reality—unreal realism. . . ." [5]

In their longing to escape the ugly reality of their actual lives the Mannons yearn for release in love untainted by pride and sin, and in death itself. O'Neill suggests this longing with three principal symbols—the South Sea islands, the fused mother-images—Marie and Christine (Clytemnestra)—and the sea chanty sung at intervals by Seth, the gardener—the Silenus who leads the chorus of townspeople. The islands represent "release, peace, security, beauty, freedom of conscience, sinlessness, etc.—longing for the primitive—and mother-symbol—yearning for pre-natal non-competitive freedom from fear. . . ." [6] The same spirit had animated Marie, whose pagan, life-loving attitude still lingers in Christine and Lavinia, symbolized for the men in the rich, "copper-gold" hair of all these women. Christine's acceptance of sexuality has been embittered by Ezra's Puritanism—distorted into a possessive passion; but to her husband, lover, and children, she still represents release and sinlessness. Even to Lavinia, who hates her because she "stole all love from me when I was born," Christine is still the longed-for mother, as well as the image of herself, Lavinia, as giver and lover. Of the third symbol of release, the sea chanty, *Shenandoah*, O'Neill says in a cryptic note ". . . its simple sad rhythm of hopeless sea longing peculiarly significant—even the stupid words have striking meaning when considered in relation to the tragic events of the play." [7] The Shenandoah is the river of life, and all the Mannons love its daughter.

Since O'Neill has shifted the emphasis of the trilogy from Orestes to Electra, the changes which take place in the character of Lavinia provide the most fruitful subject for analysis. Caught like Nina Leeds in the father complex, she struggles at once to realize and to escape from a self-image which is only a reflection of her soldier father. Her physical appearance tells the story:

Tall, like her mother, her body is thin, flat-breasted and angular, and its unattractiveness is accentuated by her plain black dress. Her movements are stiff and she carries herself with a wooden, square-shouldered, military bearing. She has a flat dry voice and a habit of snapping out her words like an officer giving orders. But in spite of these dissimilarities one is immediately struck by her facial resemblance to her mother. ("Homecoming," Act I, *Plays*, II, p. 10)

This "facial resemblance," the mask of the mother in Lavinia, will have its moment of fulfillment, but only briefly, until God the Father's lightning strikes again.

The father, Ezra, embodies the characteristics of the family which constitute their fate—pride, Puritanism, and a strong sense of vindictive justice. (He was Judge Mannon, before he became Brigadier-General Mannon.) Because of his ingrown egotism and his guilty attitude toward sex, Ezra does not, at the beginning of the play, know how to love. Desire for his wife takes the form of brutal and clumsy lust. Not until he has known the comradeship of other men on the battlefield and has seen death, does he become aware of the signifiance of love and life:

Death made me think of life. Before that life had only made me think of death. . . . That's always been the Mannon's way of thinking. They went to the white meeting house on Sabbaths and meditated on death. Life was a dying. Being born was starting to die. Death was being born. ("Homecoming," Act III, *Plays*, II, pp. 53–54)

Ironically, his ability to love and his insight into life come to Ezra only when he returns home to Christine's hatred and his own death.

Christine has fallen in love with Adam Brant, the son of Marie Brantôme. When Ezra is in the throes of a heart attack, Christine deliberately withholds his medicine. To the outside world, Ezra appears to have died from natural causes; Lavinia, however, discovers her mother's guilt. She plans her vengeance—driven not only by the Mannon sense of justice and her love for her father, but by her frustrated love for Adam (who resembles her father) and hatred and jealousy of her mother. Since Christine has "stolen" the love of both men from Lavinia, the fitting retaliation for Lavinia is not to take her mother's life, but to take from her the love which is her life. At Lavinia's instigation, Orin murders Adam Brant. Christine takes her own life, and after Christine's suicide the spirit of vindictiveness and death in the Mannons seems to be temporarily satisfied, and Lavinia can come to life. She takes on all the attributes of her mother:

She seems a mature woman, sure of her feminine attractiveness. Her brown-gold hair is arranged as her mother's had been. . . . The movements of her body now have the feminine grace her mother's had possessed. ("The Haunted," Act I, Sc. ii, *Plays*, p. 139)

Now, at perhaps her guiltiest, she has lost her sense of sin and death. Her father's ghost in Lavinia has now been placated; like him, she could find life only after experience of death.

And as Lavinia assumes the characteristics of the mother, Orin takes on those of his father. He even wears a beard and walks "like a tin soldier." Together they take a trip to the East, stopping at the South Sea islands. Orin

watches Lavinia's new sexuality with puritanical disap-
proval—and jealousy. He feels that he and Lavinia have
actually *become* their father and mother: "Can't you see
I'm now in Father's place and you're Mother? . . . I'm
the Mannon you're chained to!" ("The Haunted," Act II,
Plays, II, p. 154)

To complete the symbolic incest pattern representing
the lonely Mannons' introversion and their narcissistic inability to love any but another Mannon, Orin falls in love
with his sister. The same duality of love and loathing for
oneself and its reflection in another which has always
dominated Mannon relationships now governs this one.
Orin hates Lavinia as much as he desires her; she has
become to him what the Furies were to Orestes, a constant
reminder of guilt, driving him toward madness. He wants
to become her lover in order to force her to share his guilt.
"How else can I be sure you won't leave me? You would
never dare leave me—then! You would feel as guilty then
as I do! . . ." Lavinia, both fascinated and repelled, shouts
her hatred at him: "I hate you! You're too vile to live!
You'd kill yourself if you weren't such a coward!"

With these words Lavinia has committed her last murder. When Orin shoots himself Lavinia's last illusion of her
own innocence begins to crumble. The Puritan conscience
(or superego or father-god), from which she has found
release in identification with the mother, now reasserts
itself. She shouts defiance at the portraits of her ancestors,
". . . I'm Mother's daughter—not one of you! . . ." but
even as she does so, the Mannon pride claims its own. The
feminine Lavinia now "squares her shoulders, with a return of the abrupt military movement copied from her
father which she had of old—as if by the very act of dis-

owning the Mannons she had returned to the fold—and marches stiffly from the room." ("The Haunted," Act III, *Plays*, II, p. 168)

Lavinia makes one more desperate effort to reach from behind her mask of death toward life. She begs her childhood sweetheart, the innocent, untempted, and unsuspicious Peter, to marry her. Even as she pleads with him, however, she knows that the dead have not forgotten, and will not rest until justice has been performed. She must pay for their lives with her own, not in the easy expiation of actual death—that would be the release for which she has always longed—but in a return to the living death which is the Mannon fate, and which, as always, is to be accomplished by the Mannon pride. She tells Peter goodbye, as Seth, the gardener, sings the refrain,

> Oh, Shenandoah, I can't get near you
> Way-ay, I'm bound away—

LAVINIA: . . . I'm not bound away—not now, Seth. I'm bound here—to the Mannon dead! (*She gives a dry little cackle of laughter and turns as if to enter the house.*)

SETH: Don't go in there, Vinnie!

LAVINIA: Don't be afraid. I'm not going the way Mother and Orin went. That's escaping punishment. And there's no one left to punish me. I'm the last Mannon. I've got to punish myself! Living alone with the dead is a worse act of justice than death or prison! ("The Haunted," Act IV, *Plays*, II, p. 178)

When Lavinia "pivots sharply on her heel and marches woodenly into the house, closing the door behind her," the tension between love and pride, life and death, is dissolved; only pride and death remain. Violated order has been restored; the trap of self has finally and with finality claimed its inevitable prey.

The fatal forces at work in *Mourning Becomes Electra* can be and have been traced to Jung, to Freud, and to the popularization of a psychoanalytic study of one hundred married couples, *A Research in Marriage* by G. V. Hamilton (New York, 1929). The popular version was *What's Wrong with Marriage?* by G. V. Hamilton and Kenneth Macgowan.*

Whatever the clinical parallels, however, O'Neill has presented them not as pathology, but as tragedy. The neurotic struggle still differs in this play, as it has in others, from normal and effective human striving in that it is intrapsychic. It is a destructive prototype, within the mind, of battles which in healthy men are waged chiefly against outside forces. To O'Neill it has the same dignity, the same dramatic and tragic universality, as any struggle whatever.

But to place within the psyche a struggle which normally goes on between the psyche and other forces makes a difference on the stage, as it does in real life. That difference is clarified, I think, in Aristotle's famous remarks on Tragedy in *The Poetics:*

. . . Tragedy is the imitation of an action; and an action implies personal agents, who necessarily possess certain distinctive qualities both of character and thought; for it is by these that we qualify actions themselves. . . .

. . . the Plot is the imitation of the action:—for by plot I

* This source was suggested by Doris Alexander, in "Psychological Fate in *Mourning Becomes Electra*" (*PMLA,* LXVIII [Dec. 1953], pp. 923–934), and by W. D. Sievers in *Freud on Broadway* (New York, 1955). According to Sievers, it is possible that O'Neill himself may have been one of the original case studies.

here mean the arrangement of incidents. . . . But most important of all, is the structure of the incidents. For Tragedy is an imitation, not of men, but of an action and of life, and life consists in action, and its end is a mode of action, not a quality. Now character determines men's qualities, but it is by their actions that they are happy or the reverse. Dramatic action, therefore, is not with a view to the representation of character: character comes in as subsidiary to the actions. Hence the incidents and the plot are the end of tragedy; and the end is the chief thing of all.[8]

The term "action" has been defined and interpreted on many levels; I prefer here, however, to limit its meaning, as I think Aristotle does, to the totality of incidents which constitute the plot, and to preserve the distinction between plot and character. Plot, of course, need not mean a series of violent physical actions or events. Certainly changes in relationships between characters, whether the result of words (dialogue) or deeds, can be considered plot or action. According to Aristotle, the aim of the action should be not a "quality," but a "mode of action"—which I take to mean a consequent development of or variation upon the original action in which some interpretation of the original may be implied. In the Greek and Elizabethan tragedies the sequence of events originates with the determination of the protagonist to accomplish an aim or "end"—to become an all-powerful king, say, or to avenge a murdered father. He may achieve his aim with ironic, direful results, or he may fall victim to forces within or without himself which finally defeat him, but somewhere in the process (not always at the end of the play or even at its climax) the truth about himself and his relation to the action is revealed to him. This revelation of the self is essential to the depth and significance of a Greek or Elizabethan tragedy, but it is not an end in itself. The "epiphany" is a step in the action of the play, necessarily a crucial step leading to another "mode of action"; that is, it is an event of vital importance, but it grows out of events and leads to further events different in kind from those which preceded it. In O'Neill's plays, however, this self-revelation is the one end and aim of all the action; its purpose is not to lead to further action, but to solve the mystery of the self. The end of such a search for self is not a "mode of action," but a "quality"—a change in character.

An O'Neill protagonist is not compelled to make choices between alternate actions in order to accomplish another action; he must make a choice between alternate images of the self in order to discover the real self—which he often fails to do. Certainly he performs acts—if nothing else, he antagonizes other characters who are engaged in their own search for self, and it is in this conflict that the plot of many of O'Neill's plays consists. But the conflict with others is only a by-product of the protagonist's conflict with himself. He must solve that, must find his integrated self, before he can engage in purposeful action.

Perhaps the search for self, and for a social and moral order to which he can "belong," is really an "imitation of an action and of life" more appropriate to twentieth-century man than the imitations of more concrete outward action in the classic tragedies. Greek and Elizabethan characters acted within a known framework of value and order; we have neither, and the search for these has been the most consistent theme in modern literature. For drama, however, this modern dilemma poses artistic problems which Aristotle foretold in his insistence on the subjection of character to plot. The imitation on the stage of a mental process is after all not exactly the same as the imitation of an action. Mental processes become action only when they are dramatized—literally "acted out." The danger is that instead of a play, we may have a series of dialogues and monologues in preparation for an action which never takes place or in retrospective evaluation of action long since past. O'Neill succumbs to this danger more in *Strange Interlude* than in *Mourning Becomes Electra,* where—thanks to Aeschylus—he has a more substantial plot framework. But action in the later plays moves further and further inward until it is completely submerged in the characters' psyches—and plot is submerged in the portrayal of character.

The Aristotelian definition of character provides another link between classic tragedy and O'Neill's modern psychological drama. Character, according to Aristotle, is "ethos." It is "that which reveals moral purpose, showing what kind of things a man chooses or avoids." [9] The tragic hero brings about his own destruction through some flaw, "some error or frailty" in his character—in the self. He is free to choose his course of action, but within the limitations of the structure of the self with its flaw.

The *ethos* or moral purpose of an O'Neill character is to perpetuate or strengthen an illusion about himself. This moral purpose often runs counter to another lifelong aim, which is to discover himself. The illusion is, of course, a false self-image substituted for the real self, the latter being unconsciously hated and rejected by the character. This self-hatred and the consequent pursuit of illusion constitute the tragic flaw which destroys him.

While Aristotle does not specify the nature of the flaw

in the *Poetics,* we know that the archetypal tragic cere-
monies pictured it as *hubris,* resulting in destruction
through *Nemesis:* the swelling of the year-daemon with
seasonal plenty to such excess that the gods must kill him
in order that the yearly cycle may begin again. In the
highly developed tragedy that sprang from this ritual the
excess of *hubris* is interpreted as pride, as insolence toward
the inevitable, toward the gods—the same presumption
to Godhead which Christianity calls the sin of pride.
This need not be the obvious pride of the boaster; it
usually takes the more subtle form of mistaken confidence
in one's ability to overcome fated barriers. The bitter paradox, of course, is that the very attempt to transcend finite
limitations, itself a form of aspiration to Godhead, gives
man's struggle dignity, and his downfall grandeur. In this
concept of the fall through fatal pride, the threads of the
neurotic and the ethical, the personal and the universal
may be drawn together.

For the pride which in the Greek theater brought inevitable destruction by jealous gods is analogous to that
compulsion to attain the impossible which in a *life situation* causes destruction of the self, and which we call "neurotic." Aristotle considered the pride of the tragic hero
neither pure virtue nor "vice or depravity," but a flaw, an
"error or frailty" in the character of "a man like ourselves." [10] Neurotic pride is not pride as a virtue any
more than is the classic *hubris.* It is not that felt assumption of human dignity that enables most people who are
not tragic heroes to live cautiously and die in bed, nor is it
the righteous pride of one who sacrifices his life for a noble
cause. Neurotic pride is the flaw which makes the life of
a real person not an action, but a self-destructive imitation

of an action. The neurotic is an actor in a tragedy taking place within his own mind—vital, agonizing, tense, but self-created and divorced from objective reality.

The pride of O'Neill's characters may be neurotic, but it follows still the blinding, destructive pattern of *hubris*. Without it, there would have been no downfall for Nina and Lavinia—just as to know, accept, and control his flaw would prevent the downfall of any tragic hero. The failure to do so can no more escape retribution than any other flaw in character. If the hero does not know himself, fate will force the knowledge upon him. And with self-knowledge comes self-criticism: that evaluation of motives which results in guilt and responsibility. For the neurotic, self-knowledge may reveal the subconscious self-hatred which generated the illusory self-image in the first place; then on a conscious level the hatred can be satisfied, the self can be punished and finally accepted; justice can be accomplished and the protagonist can find peace at last.

Obviously, we see this process taking place with Lavinia, whose final acceptance of responsibility and guilt leads her to the inevitable conclusion that the only fitting punishment for the hated self must be inflicted by itself. Is not this principle at the very heart of the paradox posed by classic tragedy, that although the hero's destruction seems to be determined by fate (here by hereditary neurosis), he still takes responsibility for that destruction? Even though he may have had no control over that self which with its flaw determined his destiny, he still considers that self free; he still assumes responsibility for his actions and accepts their consequences. At the moment of self-knowledge, predestined Oedipus blinds himself in symbol of his lifelong blindness; Orestes welcomes the persecution of the Furies, although he was fated to murder his mother; Lear beats at the gates that let his folly in and his dear judgment out—and does not ask how he came to be made so foolish; and Othello smites the poor, deluded Moor of Venice, never questioning the drives within himself that created his delusion.

The problem of responsibility applied to Nina and Lavinia makes the difference between the qualities of *Strange Interlude* and *Mourning Becomes Electra* as tragedies. Nina is the victim of her neurosis or (as Doris Alexander points out) of the Schopenhauer Will to Live. While there is ethical justice in her final defeat in the sense that her egotism has destroyed her, Nina never achieves the self-understanding and consequent acknowledgment of guilt which would give the play or her character tragic proportions. She finally achieves peace, but only through exhaustion.

Lavinia's struggle is equally fated, equally hopeless, but in her the case history of a neurotic has been translated into the universal symbols of tragedy. The house of Mannon *is* the tragic flaw of its occupants. It represents the Mannon self; its walls are those of the pride system, that cell of mirrored ego-images from which no Mannon can escape alive. The outside world is only a distant threat of invasion or a vague promise of freedom; "true, fated reality" lies inward, behind the façade, behind the mask.

Mourning Becomes Electra demonstrates that in this inner world, true tragic drama may be acted. When Lavinia understands the justice of her fate and walks back into the house of self, she dramatizes her self-recognition. O'Neill has fulfilled the requirements of drama by symbolizing in literal *action* the significance and dignity of

Lavinia's tragic downfall. No stage effect, no rhapsodic chant of earth god or goddess, no mystical vision is necessary here. All follows logically and inevitably from the events of the play. O'Neill is closer here, I think, to the spirit of archetypal tragedy than in any of those plays where he tries to make that spirit explicit—*Beyond the Horizon, The Fountain, All God's Chillun Got Wings, The Great God Brown.* The tragic justice of *Mourning Becomes Electra* is more indicative of a moral order manifesting itself in a tension between irreconcilable opposites than are any of these plays, which shout aloud their affirmation of this order. O'Neill makes no effort here to show the order as beneficent—it is impersonal, indifferent to the suffering individual. But it is a great, a powerful, an inexorable order which calls from the individual all his human heroism. In the force of Lavinia's personality and acceptance of her fate her triumph is implied, as a kind of triumph is implied in *The Hairy Ape* and *The Emperor Jones.* As Henry A. Myers has pointed out [11] the refrain of Ansky's *Dybbuk* tells the story of all tragedy:

> Why, from highest height
> To deepest depth below
> Has the soul fallen?
> Within itself, the Fall
> Contains the Resurrection.

Learning, at last, to accept a moral order in which the only consolation for suffering is inherent in the suffering itself may be the mark of a tragic hero, but what about the bewildered, alienated, unheroic man who needs a more absolute order, a resurrection beyond the fall? His intuitive "hopeless hope" will keep him searching for escape from duality—for some peaceful *via media* between the heights and depths, some end to ambivalence in integrated release from the cell of mirrored masks. And death must not be the only answer. Nina's peace ought, somehow, to come while she is actively alive. Lavinia should—somehow—be able to avoid locking the door of her Mannon self behind her.

From 1931 to 1934 O'Neill struggled with his own despair and hope in his search for the "somehow." The result was *Days Without End*, completed after eight tortured drafts, in 1934. O'Neill's only other finished work in these years represented a month's vacation from the third draft of *Days Without End*. In that month he conceived, sketched, and completed his one comedy, *Ah, Wilderness!* Even this had a serious purpose; O'Neill wanted, he said, to write

a play true to the spirit of the American large small-town at the turn of the century. Its quality depended upon atmosphere, sentiment, an exact evocation of the mood of the dead past. To me, the America which was (and is) the real America found its unique expression in such middle class families as the Millers, among whom so many of my own generation passed from adolescence to manhood.[1]

Perhaps the greatest compliment we can pay to the dramatic excellence of *Ah, Wilderness!* is to say that its objectivity makes it relatively insignificant for this study— much less significant than the deeply personal and dramatically inferior *Days Without End*. The affectionate tone of *Ah, Wilderness!* hints that O'Neill felt that there must be a way out of the trap of self—or, at least, that some people are not hopelessly tormented by the masks of themselves. Fate still springs out of the family, but it is not necessarily a tragic fate. The comedy breathes a gentle if not exulting optimism, a feeling that life isn't so bad after all—even with our neuroses.

Days Without End, however, which strives so desperately to affirm not only optimism, but faith—a positive solution to the "sickness of today"—is an unconvincing drama and a philosophical whistling in the dark. Man is still born broken, and his hope for mending is literally the grace of God.

Man's name here is John Loving, whose broken self is played by two actors rather than by one with a mask. The self called "John" is "handsome with the rather heavy, conventional type of good looks. . . ." "Loving," his double, invisible to the other characters in the play, wears a mask "whose features reproduce exactly the features of John's face—the death mask of a John who has died with a sneer of scornful mockery on his lips." (Act I, *Plays,* III, pp. 493–494)

The conflict in *Days Without End* is, of course, between these two selves. The hero begins life as a devout Catholic, loving both life and God. However, at the death of his parents, in circumstances which seemed to be unjust, he dedicates himself to hatred. The "devil of hate" to whom he has sold himself is designated by his double, called, ironically, "Loving." John seeks for some kind of faith to take the place of that which he has lost. After trying many systems of philosophy, each of which is ultimately unsatisfying, he falls in love, marries, and thinks he has found the answer in human love. However, this kind of love alone is not enough to overcome the "devil of hate," for John begins to hate his dependency on and his possession by his wife—to "hate love." He tries to free himself, to kill his love by infidelity. The result is that his "good" self is now tortured by guilt at the blasphemy of his new faith, while the "evil" self secretly wishes for his wife's death and, hating

life, for his own. His wife, divining his hatred of love and
his secret wish for her death, determines upon suicide. As
she lies dying from a partly self-induced illness, John,
faced with unbearable guilt and agony, is driven back to
the church of his parents for help. At the foot of the crucifix he begs forgiveness for his past hatred. As he does so,
his double, still arguing, grows gradually weaker, until
John, receiving a "sign" of forgiveness from Christ's figure
on the crucifix, cries out "Thou art the Way—the Truth—
the Resurrection and the Life, and he that believeth in
Thy love, his love shall never die!" At these words, the
figure of the demonic self falls dead at the foot of the
cross, and John becomes unified as John Loving. News
arrives that his wife will live, and John answers with much
the same words as those of Lazarus, "Life laughs with
God's love again! Life laughs with love!" (Act IV, Sc. ii,
Plays, III, pp. 566–567)

Days Without End is O'Neill's version of the Faust
legend. One of the *Memoranda on Masks* reads as follows:

> Consider Goethe's "Faust," which, psychologically speaking,
> should be the closest to us of all the Classics. In producing
> this play, I would have Mephistopheles wearing the Mephis-
> tophelean mask of the face of Faust. For is not the whole of
> Goethe's truth *for our time* just that Mephistopheles and Faust
> are one and the same—*are* Faust.[2]

O'Neill's psychological interpretation of the Faust-
Mephistopheles conflict is closely parallel to Horney's. The
hero has sold his soul, the real self, to Loving in exchange
for Loving's mask, the false image of himself as the cynical, all-knowing intellect. The price he pays is disintegra-

tion, the loss of true identity in the rending conflict between John, the submissive, childlike lover, and this sophisticated hater.

The only way he can recover the lost self is to relinquish the evil image—the magic of intellectual godhead which ravished Dr. Faustus. He must vanquish the force of reason in order to return to faith in intuition and emotion—the love with which, O'Neill says, God laughs.

So far, the psychological meaning of the play is completely consistent with O'Neill's view of life, but that consistency is lost when John finds his solution not only in love, but in the supernatural—in Christianity or, even more specifically, Catholicism. The melodramatic ending, when the face of Christ on the crucifix lights up, the news of Elsa's recovery arrives, and John sings his hymn of praise, was unconvincing to most audiences, and to O'Neill himself. He told Nathan that "the hero's final gesture calls for alteration." Barrett Clark, who quotes O'Neill's comment, questions whether O'Neill meant the dramatic gesture or the " 'mental' gesture in returning to the Catholic faith."

O'Neill meant both. This was the very conclusion he had tried to avoid from the time when the play was conceived as a sequel to *Dynamo*. Originally, under its first title, *Without Ending of Days,* it was intended as the second play in a trilogy of which *Dynamo* was the first. (The third, never written, was to have been called *It Cannot be Mad.*) *Days Without End* is almost as desperate and hysterical in its search for faith in the supernatural as is the hero of his *Dynamo* in his effort to find solace in materialism. In many of O'Neill's earlier plays (especially *Welded*), the solution to the dilemma of integration is a

Christian one in the sense that self-sacrifice and acceptance of the tragic opposites of life is an "Imitation of Christ"— Christ's example and his humanity are central. In *Days Without End,* however, acceptance of formal Christianity is the only redemption.

O'Neill knew that John Loving's Kierkegaardian leap to "faith which resolves contradictions" was itself a contradiction of the steadfast belief in life solutions to life problems which O'Neill had maintained in all his previous work. Even when the answer was a mystical one, O'Neill had always interpreted that mysticism as a psychological phenomenon, not a supernatural one. He had been disillusioned early in the Catholicism which, as his parents' religion, represented his parents to him. In the autobiographical *Long Day's Journey Into Night* he defines his mother's Catholicism as an escape from reality, back to an illusory child's world of innocence and peace. His father's Catholicism (in that play) is mechanical and dogmatic; his pride in it serves only to mask feelings of social inferiority.

Whatever unconscious sense of a renegade's guilt may have dogged O'Neill, it was still for him just another source of alienation, another symbol of his failure "to belong." The Church could, theoretically, provide absolution, security, love, one-ness—but only for true believers. O'Neill could never believe, but consciously or not he had been tempted. In the manuscript notes and drafts [3] of *Days Without End* he has left us a fascinating record of the temptation, of the struggle with his own defenses, of his resistance and ambivalence. Follow these and you will see him at every turn rejecting the supernatural for the natural, while each step only brings him closer to his final reluctant and skeptical capitulation.

The very earliest notes for a play to be entitled either *On to Hercules* or *Without Ending of Days* begin with a Jungian analysis of the hero (here called Russell), who finally commits suicide. O'Neill's manuscript jottings for the end of the play read in part as follows:

Mother worship, repressed and turned morbid, ends by becoming Death-love and longing—thus it is statue of Virgin and child, identification of mother and Elsa with Her, himself with child, longing for reunion with them through Mother Goddess that really drives him to suicide before statue of Virgin —while at the same time it is his old resentment against mother, against Elsa as mother substitute (infidelity) that keeps him from giving in to Catholicism—longing, confession. . . .

In another early note (dated November 29, 1931), when O'Neill had decided to call the play *Without Ending of Days,* we find him taking a further step toward the Christian solution, but with reservations:

Make (if possible) religion less definitely Catholic. At the end Russell does not commit suicide, nor does he arrive at faith in the supernatural—what does come to him in the church is a sudden mark [?] of identity, brotherhood with Christ, the man, this Son of Man crucified heroically on the Cross of Life —and this gives him courage to go on, a yea-saying of bound [?] submission to inevitable fate, a conviction that this symbol of Man accepting crucifixion in order to save men from themselves is a proof of the spiritual nobility which can be attained and which can make life a noble end in itself.

This is Christianity in the sense in which O'Neill usually refers to it, as symbol and example; nevertheless, he was uncomfortable even in this carefully qualified suggestion of salvation. In the first completed version of the play (the one O'Neill calls the fourth draft) he discards the Christian or Catholic solution altogether. Elsa dies, and Loving is not saved, but ends cursing God, with neither love nor faith to sustain him.

LOVING: (*Chokingly*) She's—dead? (*The doctor nods without speaking. Loving stares at Elsa's face with a horrible anguish*) Dead! (*Then suddenly a frightful rage convulses his face and he shakes his fists above him as if he were aware of some malign murderous fate in the air*) I curse you, God damn you! I curse you.

STILLWELL: (*Sharply*) Loving! Stop it!

LOVING: (*Stares at him bewilderedly—then flings his arms about the dead woman and pulls her to him, pressing his face to her breast, sobbing hysterically*) Elsa! Elsa!

The Faust motif with the Mephistophelean double is introduced in the fifth draft, or the second complete manuscript version of the play. Here John's disintegration becomes explicit in his portrayal as two men. He finds his integration, however, not in faith, but in death. Only in the final throes of the death-struggle with himself (Loving) does he gain insight into the meaning of the crucified Christ as poor broken and divided man, but it is too late for this knowledge to save him. His last speech before the crucifix is: "Oh Son of Life, oh Brother, I see now! Forgive my blindness! Forgive thy poor damned fool!"

So far the play has progressed from "Mother-worship" and "Death-love," through renunciation and defiance of God, to the concept of integration through Christ's example. In the sixth draft—or the third complete manuscript—O'Neill takes another step toward his ultimate solution. John becomes integrated, alive, as John Loving. He curses God first, as in the first complete version, but at the moment of cursing realizes that he believes in God and has always believed and that his hatred should have been love. "But if I curse, I must believe! I must have always believed! (*He gives a laugh that is half sob*) I see now! I see! Oh Lord, forgive thy poor damned fool!" Elsa lives, as in the final version, and John's last speech is almost that of the version which O'Neill eventually published. "I know. Love lives forever. There is a God—who laughs with love!"

In the next version—actually the last, except for a few minor changes—the earlier conception of Christ as a symbol of suffering man merges with the belief in the existence of God, becoming a belief in Christ as God. The progression from faith in the subconscious, "the mother of all gods and heroes," to faith in Christianity, in Catholicism, is complete.

If O'Neill had been writing in his usual vein, the cessation of strife between the two selves of John Loving would have meant the ending of all struggle, movement, and growth for him, or death. Loving is a "finder," but he does not discover acceptance of inevitable disunity; he thinks he has found unity. O'Neill was unhappy about Loving's final gesture because it appeared to be conclusive, to suggest that one can escape the tragic tension between opposites and still lead a rich life. John's return to the faith constitutes a withdrawal from life, and no amount of protestation in the form of stage symbolism nor of exclamatory affirmation can convince us otherwise. Nothing could make this clearer than comparison of *Days Without*

End with Strindberg's play on the same subject, with essentially the same conclusion, *To Damascus.*

The conflicting selves of Strindberg's protagonist are represented by several characters—the Stranger, the Beggar, the Doctor, the Tempter. The first three of these form a conglomerate character comparable to John, while the Tempter is the voice of rationality and experience—Loving. There is even an all-knowing "Confessor," comparable to Father Baird of *Days Without End.* The protagonist has struggled with the same problems in his search for significance in life as has John, seeking the solution first in one political or scientific creed, then in another, and has reached the same crucial point—he finally believes that the answer is in the love of a woman, but is unable to accept the ambivalent nature of love in which resentment of her possessiveness and his dependence breeds hate. (Here Strindberg, of course, makes the woman a more active source of evil than does O'Neill, but even Strindberg sees the blame as, on the whole, equally divided.) The dramatic ending of Strindberg's play is different from O'Neill's, in that Strindberg's hero renounces earthly love completely and goes into a monastery—the only place where he can find integration of his divided selves—where portraits may be painted with one face, because there "we have no opinions, we believe." His solution is a frank withdrawal from life—a symbolic death. In the final scene of the play, a few seconds before the curtain falls on the entire trilogy, the Stranger in a dialogue with his double, the Tempter, affirms the tragic opposites of love and life, but denies his own strength to endure them and withdraws into the monastery. Every word of this finale sheds light on the similarity of, and the deviation between, the two plays:

(*A woman, with a baptized child, passes across the stage.*)
THE TEMPTER: See, there is a little mortal, destined to suffer!
THE STRANGER: Poor child!
THE TEMPTER: The first chapter in the history of man. (*A pair of newly-weds across the stage.*) And there—the loveliest— the bitterest! Adam and Eve in Paradise, in eight days in Hell, in fourteen, once more in Paradise. . . .
THE STRANGER: The loveliest! The most illuminating! . . . The first, the only, the last thing that gives value to life! . . . Once I sat in the sun—a spring day, on a veranda—under the first green tree, and a little halo crowned a head, and a white veil lay like a faint morning-mist over a face, which was not that of a human being. . . . Then darkness came!
THE TEMPTER: Where from?
THE STRANGER: From the light itself! . . . If not from the light then I don't know.
THE TEMPTER: It must have been a shadow, because shadow requires light, while darkness. . . .
THE STRANGER: Stop! Or we will never come to the end!
(*The Confessor and The Chapter appear in procession.*)
THE TEMPTER: Goodby! (*He disappears.*)
THE CONFESSOR: (*with a large black pall*). God, give him eternal peace!
THE CHOIR: And may the everlasting light shine upon him!
THE CONFESSOR: (*wraps The Stranger in the pall*). May he rest in peace!
THE CHOIR: Amen! [4]

Like Strindberg's Stranger, O'Neill knew that the only escape from the oppositions of light and shadow, from the fluctuations of the natural cycle, is in death. In *To Damascus,* of course, this is a ritual death, signifying a death to the world and rebirth in faith. O'Neill, prior to *Days Without End,* had always assumed that faith was itself a phenomenon of this world, the expression of a universal psychological need. Belief in the supernatural was an illusion, a "pipe dream" to keep men alive when other values were gone. He returned to this conception in his subsequent work, and never betrayed it again.

In 1939, six years after *Days Without End,* O'Neill completed *The Iceman Cometh;* in 1940–41, *Long Day's Journey Into Night,* and in 1943, *A Moon for the Misbegotten* and *A Touch of the Poet.* During the same general period —from about 1934 to 1943—O'Neill had been hard at work on two long cycles of plays to be called *A Tale of Possessors Self-Dispossessed* and *By Way of Obit.* Of the first cycle [1] he completed first drafts of three double-length plays, *The Greed of the Meek, And Give Me Death,* and *More Stately Mansions.* Dissatisfied with the early drafts of these plays and too ill to undertake drastic revision,

O'Neill destroyed the first two. Although he had intended the destruction also of *More Stately Mansions,* a typescript of that play survives (the manuscript version was destroyed with the other two plays). Of the second cycle, *By Way of Obit,* O'Neill completed only one one-act play, entitled *Hughie,* still extant but unpublished.

At one time O'Neill had placed *A Touch of the Poet* fifth in the *Possessors* cycle, but when he abandoned the latter he considered his last four plays to be a related series,[2] arranged in the following order: *The Iceman Cometh, A Moon for the Misbegotten, A Touch of the Poet,* and *Long Day's Journey Into Night.* The exact composition dates of these and the cycle plays are far from clear; some had been begun years before—*A Touch of the Poet* in 1928.[3] We do know, however, that between completion of *Days Without End* and this final group of plays about ten years had elapsed in which O'Neill's thinking underwent a change that reflected the frustrations of the intervening years.

O'Neill returned in these last plays to acceptance of struggle and flight as inseparable from and intrinsic to the life process. Now there is no way out but death. The struggle in these plays is essentially the same as it had always been in his work: the conscious intellect at war with the unconscious drives, the laceration of love and hate in every close human relationship, and the desperate search for self among the masks. Flight from the struggle is still in the pursuit of one of these illusory masks—but here we see a difference.

At last O'Neill had come face to face with the inevitable question: What happens when, long before the end of the play, the fugitive becomes clearly conscious that flight is futile and the self-image false? When he learns that *all* self-images are illusions, and that furthermore they are projected by a self which is worthless, if it exists at all? Then the self and its ideal are equal—and both equal to zero. Instead of a pull from the self to the self-conception, resulting in action (wasteful though that action may be), we have a perfect equilibrium, resulting in paralysis. Then, indeed,

> . . . the odds is gone,
> And there is nothing left remarkable
> Beneath the visiting moon.

The theme of *The Iceman Cometh* is the death that re-sults—the "iceman" who comes—when the self-images which keep the characters alive become known to them as mirage. The action takes place in "Hope's back room," the back room and a section of the bar of Harry Hope's saloon.* Here fifteen derelicts keep themselves alive on alcohol and the "pipe dream" that they have been or some day will be respectable. They all know, at least uncon-sciously, the truth about themselves and each other, but they know, too, the vital necessity of illusion. So each accepts the other at his own evaluation and demands the same acceptance. As long as this state of things persists, as

---

* Harry Hope's is a composite of Jimmy the Priest's and the Golden Swan (or Hell Hole, as it was known), a bar and hangout in Greenwich Village, now defunct. The characters of *The Iceman Cometh* are drawn from O'Neill's acquaintances at both these establishments. Terry Carlin, a seventy-year-old ex-Anarchist and friend of O'Neill from the Province-town-Greenwich Village days, was the original of Larry Slade; Rocky, the bartender in *Iceman,* is probably Lefty, bartender at the Golden Swan; Hugo Kalmar, the old radical of *Iceman,* is based on one Hypolyte Havel.

it does throughout the first act (nearly half the play), the characters are treated as comic. Their self-deceptions are ridiculous but not unlovable affectations. It is in the second act that, as O'Neill said, "the comedy breaks up and the tragedy comes on."

The commentator on the action and the actual protagonist of the play is Larry Slade, an aging ex-Anarchist who has long since withdrawn from the Movement and from life. In Act I Larry is comparatively happy. He has an image of himself as the philosopher-bum who observes life from the grandstand and waits only for death. He is proud that he can see what the others cannot: that "the lie of a pipe-dream is what gives life to the whole misbegotten mad lot of us, drunk or sober. . . . Mine are all dead and buried behind me. What's before me is the comforting fact that death is a fine long sleep and I'm damned tired, and it can't come too soon for me." (Act I, *Plays*, III, p. 578)

Yet, Larry's final disillusionment is still to come, in the person of young Parritt, the eighteen-year-old ex-Anarchist who has betrayed the Movement and his own mother, whom Larry once loved. (In fact, the context hints that Parritt is Larry's son.) Disillusion comes for the others in the person of Hickey (Theodore Hickman), the traveling salesman whose success they all envy.

Hickey arrives at the bar on Harry Hope's birthday, an occasion for one of his periodical binges, but instead of the gay and dissolute Hickey they all expect, he is serious and sober. He announces the reason for the change: He has at last found peace by facing the truth about himself. Gradually he shames his listeners into believing that they, too, will find peace if they destroy their illusions and see them-

selves as they really are. He persuades all except Larry
to go forth into the daylight and attempt the social re-
habilitation they have always promised themselves. One
by one, however, they crawl back to the bar the next day,
broken and defeated by inevitable failure. They have
faced the truth, but it has robbed them of the last, pitiful
trace of hope.

Now not even liquor can make them happy; their old
friendships turn to antagonisms. Hickey realizes that his
plan has failed, and in trying to explain the failure to himself and to them he reveals that he attained his state of
"peace" by killing his wife, Evelyn.

Hickey has convinced himself that he killed his wife
because he loved her and wanted to spare her unhappiness
over his uncontrollable drunkenness and dissipation—but
as he speaks, his real motive comes through. He hated
Evelyn because no matter what he did she always forgave
him, never punished him, was always faithful. His running
gag with the boys at Hope's had been that Evelyn was
betraying him "in the hay with the iceman," but this was
only his own wishful thinking. She never gave him even
this relief from his own guilt. Hickey killed Evelyn because that was the only way he could free himself from
her eternal forgiveness and achieve the ultimate in self-
punishment. For him, to commit murder was to commit
suicide. He has already called the police at the time of his
confession.

When the police have arrived, however, and Hickey is
concluding his story, his guilt becomes too much for him to
face. Ironically, he creates his own pipe dream by persuad-
ing himself that he was insane at the moment of the murder. Hickey's illusion is a blessing to his friends, for it

restores their own. Now they can go back to their bottles, convinced that they knew Hickey was insane all the time and faced reality only to humor him.

But Larry cannot go back. He must listen to Parritt's confessions—in dramatic antiphony to Hickey's—of his hatred of his mother (caused chiefly by jealousy of her many lovers) which led him to betray her to life imprisonment. Parritt has already resolved upon suicide, but he forces Larry to support his resolution. After listening to Parritt's outpourings, Larry finally cries, "Go, get the hell out of life, God damn you, before I choke it out of you! . . ." Parritt is relieved and grateful: "Thanks, Larry. I just wanted to be sure. I can see now it's the only possible way I can ever get free from her. . . . It ought to comfort Mother a little, too. . . . She'll be able to say, 'Justice is done! So may all traitors die!' . . ."

The mother-spirit has destroyed another of her sons.

When Larry hears Parritt fall from the fire escape, "A long forgotten faith returns to him for a moment. . . ." At least Parritt had the courage of his conviction. But the death of Parritt is the death of Larry's last illusion about himself. "He opens his eyes—with a bitter self-derision." He is no longer the philosopher, but only another down-and-out bum.

Be God, there's no hope! I'll never be a success in the grandstand—or anywhere else! Life is too much for me! I'll be a weak fool looking with pity at the two sides of everything till the day I die! . . . Be God, I'm the only real convert to death Hickey made here. From the bottom of my coward's heart I mean that now! (Act IV, *Plays*, III, pp. 726–727)

The objectivist (as Larry thought he was at first), who looks at both sides of everything until they have equal value, must be a paralyzed spectator, unable to take action in any direction; but when the "two sides" are the masks of himself and both are worthless illusions, perfectly balanced against each other, he is not even a paralyzed spectator; he is dead. In *The Iceman Cometh,* as in the earlier plays, life and the self are lost together, when the tragic tension between the selves is lost.

The two sides of himself that Larry has seen are his expansive and submissive self-images. The expansive is that of the Anarchist, the active participator in "the Movement." The submissive is seen in his drive toward self-destruction. If Larry had been able to give either of these selves the value of a reality, he would have been drawn toward one or toward the other, would have been able to act either in the direction of his political obligations or in the direction of death by suicide, as Parritt did. Since he is pulled in both directions at once, he can only withdraw from the struggle altogether and become a non-participating observer of himself as well as of life. In Jung's terms, Larry exemplifies the "equal distribution of psychic energy." In Horney's, he is the neurotic who finds a pseudosolution to conflict in "resignation: the appeal of freedom." When Larry himself discovers the unreality of his solution, there is nothing left for him but the living death which Kierkegaard called "the disconsolateness of not being able to die." Even his conception of physical death as a warm and comforting womb (the return to the Earth Mother) or as a Babylon where " 'tis cool beneath thy willow tree" is to him only another illusion. Nevertheless, death is the single solution to his dilemma, since only annihilation of the self can annihilate the dilemma. His very inability to propel himself actively toward this annihilation—to accomplish it through suicide—is also death.

The philosophical implications of Larry's position are just as interesting as the psychological. Behind Aristotle's ethical definition of character as "that which reveals moral purpose, showing what kind of things a man chooses or avoids," is the problem which exists in some degree for every self-aware person, as it does in the extreme for the neurotic: the problem of creating oneself, of forming one's own character. The preliminaries and the process of choosing, even though they may be unconscious, are as important as the choice itself and the responsibility which is its result. Larry's power of choice is brought to a standstill because he cannot accomplish the preparation for it. His is the problem of projecting value in a world devoid of absolutes—the "existential" dilemma: man's chief struggle is not with Something but with Nothing, not with Evil but with the valuelessness that is neither good nor evil. Once he has overcome this Nothing, has created his values, man is then free to act according to them (or even, knowingly, contrary to them), but he is completely responsible both for the values and the actions predicated upon them. Such utter self-contingency can be paralyzing; it provides freedom, but it is that terrifying freedom from which, as Erich Fromm points out, most of us feel compelled to escape.

In defense of this philosophy as a "humanism" Sartre has pointed out that it is as positive as it is negative—as hopeful as it is despairing—in that each man has not only the responsibility, but the opportunity, to create his own destiny, and that each individual is ultimately responsible for the destiny of mankind as a whole. O'Neill has not only placed Larry in the existential dilemma, but has made him see and live both sides of the dilemma itself. In his youth Larry dedicated himself to Anarchism, an affirmation of nothingness and chaos and of man's freedom to create his destiny; but in his old age he sees anarchy's opposite face, that negation which we call despair.

The Iceman Cometh was written in 1939 during a period of deep depression and anxiety for O'Neill which he attributed to the impending war. The most revealing of his statements about his mental attitude at this time is in one of his letters to Clark, in 1941. O'Neill had temporarily stopped work on the cycle ". . . pending a return of sanity and future to our groggy world. . . . So much has happened without and within, since I started to write it. The stories of the separate plays aren't affected much, but the vision of life that binds them into a whole has bogged down in shifting uncertainties. . . ." [4]

Certainly O'Neill recorded those shifting uncertainties in *Iceman.* They had obliterated the philosophy of *Bound East for Cardiff,* which O'Neill had called "the germ of the spirit, life-attitude, etc., of all my more important future work." In this early play O'Neill had seen man as the courageous hero of his tragic life struggle; now, in 1941, man had proved himself a coward and an idiot, clinging for life to the very delusions which had unmanned him. He is an object of disgust, but withal pitiful.

The years in O'Neill's life closest in mood to the despair of 1939 and the following years were those of 1911 and 1912. O'Neill had come again to the hopelessness and death longing that in those months of destitution at Jimmy the Priest's had driven him to attempt suicide. One of O'Neill's roommates at Jimmy's, a press agent named Jimmy Beith, killed himself in a jump from a window.[5] A month or so afterward O'Neill tried to end his life by means of an overdose of veronal, but was discovered in time and revived at Bellevue. That act was the young O'Neill's culminating answer to all the frustrations and confusions of his life—the failure to find himself, the guilts and tensions within the family, illness, an unhappy marriage. (In 1912 he was divorced from Kathleen Jenkins, mother of Eugene, Jr., whom he had married in 1909.) There is a bitter reference to the attempted suicide in *Long Day's Journey Into Night,* where O'Neill links it to the rumor that his grandfather had taken his own life. Again O'Neill is interpreting the drive toward self-destruction as a manifestation of the family fate. Correct or not, the interpretation was sadly corroborated in the suicide of his own son, Eugene, Jr.

So it was that on the arid plateau of *The Iceman Cometh* the only meaningful reality to O'Neill was that of his own past and the family pattern woven into that past and into the dismal present. At first he circled around biographical realism at some distance with his projected cycle of plays to be called *A Tale of Possessors Self-Dispossessed.* He intended the cycle to record the rise of an Irish family in America and its struggle to establish itself in conflict with the hostile and exploitative Yankees. Although this conflict provides the background for *A Touch of the Poet* (New Haven, 1957) the play's real theme is the same as that of *The Iceman Cometh*—the conflict between prideful illusion and shameful reality in a character who keeps his self-respect only by perpetuating the illusion.

He is Cornelius—"Con"—Melody, an Irish immigrant whose father began life as "a thievin' shebeen keeper who got rich by moneylendin' and squeezin' tenants and every manner of trick." Once wealthy, however, Con's father bought a castle on an estate in Ireland and educated his son to be a gentleman. Since Con was never completely accepted by his aristocratic schoolmates or their families, his life becomes a constant rebellion against his humble origin on one hand and the snobbery of the gentry on the other. He never is certain where he belongs. He rejects the peasant in himself and yet affirms him, but each time he becomes aware of the peasant image he is driven to deny it and to assert the image of the arrogant aristocrat. Con falls in love with a peasant girl and marries her after she becomes pregnant. Then, as Major Cornelius Melody of the British Army, he leaves her on his father's estate and goes to the Napoleonic wars. He acquires a reputation as a courageous if hotheaded young officer, but is finally forced to leave the army in disgrace after killing a fellow officer in a duel over the latter's wife.

Con emigrates with his wife, Nora, and his daughter, Sara, and sets up as a tavern-keeper in a village near Boston. As a kind of travesty of his Irish past the tavern is the center of a "country estate" which includes surrounding land and a lake. When the play opens, however, twenty years after his arrival in America, Con has failed at his trade. The family are almost destitute and the business near bankruptcy, but Con still plays the role of Major Cornelius Melody. His speech and bearing are still those of the gentleman; he rides a handsome mare and on the anniversary of the battle of Talavera dons his old uniform. The play turns on a series of tableaux in which Con stands before the mirror in his officer's scarlet coat, reciting Byron, with all the histrionics of a James O'Neill in the role of Monte Cristo.

In America Con has suffered the same alienation from self and society that he experienced in Europe. He knows he is beyond the pale of the established Boston families, but refuses to be identified with the Irish immigrants. Con has given up any real aspirations to belong to Boston society except, of course, in his dream-world. But his daughter, Sara, has not. She loves and intends to marry Simon Harford, son of a wealthy Yankee capitalist (the same who is referred to in *Moon for the Misbegotten* as "Harder," and in *Long Day's Journey* as "Harker"). Young Harford has come out to the country to meditate and write in a cabin on Melody's property. When the play opens, he is ill in a room upstairs in the tavern and is being nursed by Sara. Simon, who never appears on-stage but is described in detail by Sara, is dimly suggestive of the young O'Neill of the 1911 *Iceman* period, living sick and disconsolate over the barroom at Jimmy the Priest's. In fact, the time of *A Touch of the Poet*, ostensibly 1828, is actually, in O'Neill's mind 1911, for Melody's tavern is frequented chiefly by old derelicts, who sponge drinks by providing the Major with an audience to keep his "pipe dream" alive.

That dream is encouraged most by Con's wife, Nora, and threatened most by his daughter. *A Touch of the Poet* follows the usual O'Neill allegorical pattern. The Father is Pride, Lust, and Greed (this applies to both Melody and the elder Harford); the mother is submissive love, and the daughter—like her predecessors Nina and Lavinia—is the tormented combination of the two. The play suffers from over-exposition of this theme. Every action is explained by the characters—the word *pride* itself appears in one form or another in the text sixty-three times, usually followed by *humiliation* or *shame*. O'Neill is not satisfied with having Con act out his ridiculous and pathetic illusions, but must always make him analyze them.

Con's image of himself as the gallant officer is, of course, doomed. It awaits only a test which will destroy it and leave behind a defeated wreck worthy of the cast of *Iceman*. The test comes when the elder Harford, shocked at his son's involvement with Sara, offers to pay Con a settlement if his family will relinquish any claims on Simon and will go away. This insult, following as it does a snub by Mrs. Harford earlier in the play, so infuriates Con that he rushes to the millionaire's home to challenge him to a duel. He is promptly thrown out by Harford's servants; the whole affair degenerates into a street brawl, broken up by the police, and the final blow to Melody's pride comes when he realizes that he has disgraced himself before Harford's beautiful wife, and that his bail has been paid by Harford himself. When Melody returns to the tavern, he is no longer "the Major," but the son of the Irish shebeen-keeper. In a thick brogue he speaks of the Major as dead, caricatures his own Byronic pose, and in a final melodramatic gesture, shoots not himself, but his horse. The symbolic meaning of the action hardly needs explanation, but we have it, anyway: Sara asks her father why he killed the mare, and he answers,

Why did the Major, you mean! . . . Wasn't she the livin' reminder, so to spake, av all his lyin' boasts and dreams? He meant to kill her first wid one pistol, and then himself wid the other. But faix, he saw the shot that killed her had finished him, too. There wasn't much pride left in the auld lunatic, anyway, and seeing her die made an end av him. . . . (Act IV, *A Touch of the Poet*, pp. 168–169)

The wife, Nora, is a forgiving and browbeaten Earth-Mother, who while pitiable is still a little sickening in her mooning over the handsome husband who has spent his life abusing her. True, the Irish peasant in Con loves her in his way, but the Major despises her. She, too, analyzes herself for the audience. When Sara accuses her mother of enslaving herself to Con, Nora answers: "There's no slavery in it when you love! *Suddenly her exultant expression crumbles and she breaks down.* For the love of God, don't take the pride of my love from me, Sara, for without it what am I at all but an ugly, fat woman gettin' old and sick!" (Act I, p. 26) This is the bitter truth behind her constant submission to and forgiveness of her husband—but need we be told?

Sara represents both her father's "divil of pride" and her mother's instincts for selfless love. Toward her father she feels the ambivalence of love and hate, pride and scorn. She worships the idea of the Major—even unconsciously imitating her father's pose at times; but the very discrepancy between what her father might have been and what he is intensifies her resentment. Some of the most powerful scenes in the play are those in which father and daughter are engaged in an *agon* of hatred and self-revelation. Con sees in Sara the peasant in himself—her clumsy movements, her large hands and feet—and tortures himself and her with his jeers; on the other hand, she is the daughter of Major Melody, a lady of gentle birth, whose reputation has been threatened. Sara, for her part, must reconcile her inherited pride with her—also inherited—love. She will love Simon, but not with the slavishness of her mother's love for Con. With mixed motives of ambition and love Sara "allows" Simon to seduce her, but as she yields to him discovers the selflessness of her mother's kind of love. She, too, becomes starry-eyed and believes that at last the devil of pride in her has been overcome. "Now it's dead, thank God—and I'll make a better wife for Simon." And yet, a few seconds later, she is weeping for the death of her father's illusions; the proud Major was a part of her, too. Nora tries in her own way to comfort Sara, and she—the mother—has the closing words of the play, "Shame on you to cry when you have love. What would the young lad think of you?"

The theme of the cycle, however, is not the power of love but the transmission through the family of pride, avarice, and ruthless ambition. Simon Harford's mother has described at length the exploitative greed of the Harford family which parallels the pride and social ambition of the Melodys. There is no reason to suppose that these traits would not dominate the children of Sara and Simon. In fact, it is ironic that of the extant plays, the one in which this theme culminates is *Long Day's Journey Into Night*—never intended as part of the cycle. Its characters are the true descendants of Sara and Simon, compounded of the same illusions and greeds, and in each of them "a touch of the poet."

After a long struggle, O'Neill gave up the cycle of plays about the presumably imaginary Irish family when he found his final material in his immediate family, the subject of the posthumously published and produced *Long Day's Journey Into Night*. *A Touch of the Poet* was contrived and melodramatic, but *Long Day's Journey* is genuine drama; in O'Neill's words, a play "of old sorrow, written in tears and blood." The old sorrow was real; the play re-creates the tortured secrets of O'Neill's own family. But the importance of *Long Day's Journey* as biography is minor (most of the facts revealed in it had long been known or guessed) compared to its value as a synthesis of all we have been saying about the man and his work. It is an epilogue—a subdued, heart-rending coda sounding the themes of the entire canon. For this reason it deserves separate interpretation as the final chapter of O'Neill's career as a dramatist.

The sequel to *Long Day's Journey*, *A Moon for the Misbegotten,* continues the story of James Tyrone, Jr., who represents O'Neill's older brother, James, Jr. In *Long Day's Journey,* "Jamie" is an alcoholic, seeking constant escape from his own inadequacies and from guilt toward his younger brother and his mother. His final refuge is in lechery, but he can find satisfaction only in ugly, oversized women, the prostitutes rejected by other men, who feed his self-hatred and his need for a mother-substitute. The love affair in *A Moon for the Misbegotten* is derived from *Long Day's Journey,* which defines Jamie's love, hatred, and guilt toward his mother and the desperate longing for her which drives him to Josie in *Moon.*

If *A Moon for the Misbegotten* is a part of James, Jr.'s biography, then as biography, it is a thing of pity and terror. But as drama, it is the veriest scratching in rat's alley. The first half (actually Act I) is a crude country-bumpkin farce, taking place outside the run-down shack of a tenant farmer in Connecticut. In the second half, as in *Iceman,* "the comedy breaks up and the tragedy comes on." The change in tenor is simply a change in point of view. The setting of Act II is "the same, but with the interior of sitting room revealed"—and the interior of the characters also. Before, they were comic grotesques, seen by a detached observer; now they are revealed from their own subjective point of view as pathetic creatures of "sadness and loneliness and humiliation."

Pathos cannot save *A Moon for the Misbegotten* (New York, 1952) from the weakness of its outward situation—the theatrical cliché of clichés, for which there is no other word but corn. O'Neill added a few twists, anecdotes, and complications for interest and transition to the psychological, but the skeletal story concerns the attempt of the farmer and the farmer's daughter to save the old homestead from the clutches of a supposedly villainous landlord. To this antiquity, like insult to injury, O'Neill has added another: the vaudeville team of the big strong woman who chases a puny man around the stage with (a) a broom and (b) the threat of a smothering embrace in a pair of enormous arms and an appalling bosom. The crowning indignity is the use, as a sort of refrain, of the maudlin sob-tune, "My mother's in the baggage coach ahead." Thus the play begins with a minstrel show (there actually exists a minstrel tune that goes, "A mother was chasing her boy with a broom, she was chasing her boy 'round the room. . . .") and ends with meller-drammer. And with all his early theatrical experience and his belief that "life copies melodrama," O'Neill certainly knew what he was doing. He drops us a hint when he has Hogan, the farmer, describe his scheme for trapping the landlord (forcing him into a shotgun wedding with his daughter): "It's as old as the hills. . . . But . . . sometimes an old trick is best because it's so ancient no one would suspect you'd try it." (Act I, *A Moon for the Misbegotten*, p. 22)

As to the serious, or "subjective," side of the play, the revelations of the psychological problems of the characters fit perfectly—too perfectly—into the pattern of O'Neill's thought at this time: that balance between the opposite masks of self, that paralyzing suspension of all value, which is fatal to action and movement and signifies the end of life. This pattern is actually all there is to the play; for, whereas *The Iceman Cometh* has a story and reveals living characters in conflict with themselves and each other, the story of *A Moon for the Misbegotten* serves only as a rack on which to hang—or stretch—the unconverted symbols of neurosis.

The three central characters of this play are New England Irish, with just enough Catholicism still clinging to them to provide expressive profanity. Phil Hogan is the farmer, his daughter is Josie, and Jim Tyrone, Jr., is the landlord whose family has long owned the Hogan farm. Hogan is a buffoon with a shrewd, coarse sense of humor but a soft heart, who serves in the plot largely as a kind of *deus ex machina* to bring the lovers together. On the pretext that Tyrone is planning to sell the farm to a neighboring villainous "Standard Oil man," Hogan persuades Josie to seduce Tyrone—then to blackmail him, by forcing him either to marry her or to pay Hogan the price of the farm to avoid scandal. However, Hogan reveals later that he knew Tyrone had no intention of selling the farm, and he (Hogan) only wanted to bring the two together so that they would recognize their hidden love for each other—a rather sad piece of hokum.

The story belongs, of course, to the misbegotten lovers,

Josie, "so oversize for a woman that she is almost a freak," and Tyrone, the hopeless alcoholic, who finds, at least for one night, a mother and a lover in Josie. Unlike the men in *The Iceman Cometh*, Josie and Tyrone are protected by no lasting illusions about themselves. Josie's kindest "pipe dream" is her boast that she is a slut, who has slept with all the men in the neighborhood. But even she is aware of the truth of Jim's accusation that it is her "pride" which makes her affect this pose: that she is actually a virgin, longing to transcend her gross flesh in a spiritual love, but ashamed of this purity which seems too incongruous in a "great, ugly cow" of a woman.

When Tyrone attempts to confront Josie with this picture of her "submissive" self as a virgin, she refuses to admit the truth of the picture. To her denial Tyrone replies, "Pride is the sin by which the angels fell. Are you going to keep that up—with me?" (Act III, *A Moon for the Misbegotten*, p. 134) O'Neill knew well the close relationship between self-hatred and neurotic pride. To overcome her hatred of that empirical "oversize" self which she can see, Josie has erected a more acceptable one which at least makes her an expansive, forceful character: feeling unlovable, she proves to herself that she can make men desire her, and in that process rejects the mixture of mother and virgin which Tyrone discovers that she really is.

Tyrone reveals Josie's position and his own when he says:

You can take the truth, Josie—from me. Because you and I belong to the same club. We can kid the world but we can't fool ourselves, like most people, no matter what we do—nor escape ourselves no matter where we run away. Whether it's the bottom of a bottle, or a South Sea Island, we'd find our own ghosts there waiting to greet us—"sleepless with pale commemorative eyes," as Rossetti wrote. . . . You don't ask how I saw through your bluff, Josie. You pretend too much. . . . (Act III, *A Moon for the Misbegotten*, p. 135)

But Josie is healthy enough to see and accept her conflicting selves for what they are: to be the virgin mother to Tyrone and resume her play-acting role of neighborhood slut when he has gone. She is another Cybel, with enough earthy animal love of life to go on living in spite of her difficulties, to meet the problems of everyday life through the haze of sadness and frustration that hangs over her. She has the "hopeless hope" that springs from Cybel's assumption of the inevitability of life opposites—between which her fate is still suspended, and in which she can still find some value and motion.

For Tyrone, on the other hand, there is no hope but in oblivion. He is probably the least dramatic of any of O'Neill's protagonists. His role in the play is one long self-analysis, one endless case history of self-hatred, alienation, neurotic conflict—all within the Oedipus configuration. Tyrone wears the same two masks as Jamie in *Long Day's Journey* (and as John Loving and Dion Anthony). His ravaged face has "a certain Mephistophelean quality which is accentuated by his habitually cynical expression. But when he smiles without sneering, he still has the ghost of a former youthful, irresponsible Irish charm—that of the beguiling ne'er-do-well, sentimental and romantic." In his sodden conversations with Josie he alternates between the coarse cruelty of a disillusioned lecher and the sweetness and simplicity of a little boy crying for his mother.

Expansive at one moment, submissive at another, he does not know his real identity and withdraws from both self-images into the oblivion of drunkenness and the darkness of the womb—synonymous for him with tomb.

If the first glimpse of Tyrone reveals his disintegration within the masks of self, the second view of him is a study in self-hatred. At the end of Act II, when he has come to keep a date with Josie (and when *his* intentions are honorable, but hers are to seduce and then blackmail him), he is left for a few minutes alone on the stage.

TYRONE: (*suddenly, with intense hatred*) You rotten bastard! (*He springs to his feet—fumbles in his pockets for cigarettes —strikes a match which lights up his face, on which there is now an expression of miserable guilt. His hand is trembling so violently he cannot light the cigarette.*)

Tyrone explains his guilt to Josie and to himself in terms of his lifelong hatred of his father and love and guilty longing for his mother. During his father's lifetime Tyrone was a drunkard and a ne'er-do-well, but after his father's death he stopped drinking for his mother's sake. "It made me happy to do it. For her. Because she was all I had, all I cared about. Because I loved her."(Act III, *A Moon for the Misbegotten*, p. 146)

Then his mother became ill, and when Tyrone knew she was dying he turned to alcohol again: "I know damned well just before she died she recognized me. She saw I was drunk. Then she closed her eyes so she couldn't see, and was glad to die." (Act III, *A Moon for the Misbegotten*, p. 147)

With his mother's death, all purpose and value departed

from Tyrone's life, leaving him incapable of emotion, even of grief. He traveled across the country by train with his mother's body "in the baggage coach ahead," and spent his drunken nights with a prostitute he had picked up. Tyrone reduces his motives for this debauchery to vengeance upon his mother for leaving him. From that time on his life has been one long effort to obliterate his guilt and to punish himself not only for his behavior toward his mother, but for his feelings toward her, with their unconscious overtones of incest and hatred. Like so many of O'Neill's men, he hates the thing he loves—rebels against his dependency, then flagellates himself for having desecrated the mother-son (or man-woman) relationship.

When Tyrone comes to Josie, his one desire is for expiation. That same wronged maternal ghost who cried for vindication in *Desire Under the Elms* and *Mourning Becomes Electra* must here again be laid to rest. In Josie's maternal and redemptive love for him Tyrone at last finds forgiveness and release. When he has confessed to Josie and discovers that he is still loved in spite of the hateful self he has revealed in the confession, Tyrone is absolved. The maternal spirit has been placated; now Tyrone can sleep, now he can die. All that remains is the fulfillment of the Earth Mother's final blessing: "May you have your wish and die in your sleep soon, Jim, darling. May you rest forever in forgiveness and peace." *A Moon for the Misbegotten* takes place in September, 1923. O'Neill's brother, James, died on November 8 of that year.

Tyrone is O'Neill's last little boy lost, crying for his mother. Whether or not he actually portrays James O'Neill, Jr., the relationship between him and Josie was O'Neill's final bitter and rather immature comment on the meaning of love. On the application of this view to O'Neill himself, his wife has had the last word. In an interview at the opening of *Long Day's Journey Into Night,* Mrs. Carlotta Monterey O'Neill described "Gene's" courtship:

. . . And he never said to me, "I love you, I think you are wonderful." He kept saying, "I need you. I need you. I need you." And he did need me, I discovered. He was never in good health. He talked about his early life—that he had had no real home, no mother in the real sense, or father, no one to treat him as a child should be treated—and his face became sadder and sadder.[6]

In 1941 O'Neill completed *Long Day's Journey Into Night*. A few of his close friends were permitted to read the manuscript, but the author stipulated that the play was not to be produced or published until twenty-five years after his death. Copies were placed in the vaults of O'Neill's publisher, Random House, and in the Yale University Library (along with early drafts and notes). When reporters at the *Iceman* interview had asked him to explain the restriction, O'Neill had answered, "There is one person in it who is still alive. . . ." In February of 1956, however, three years after O'Neill's death, *Long Day's*

Journey was published with Mrs. O'Neill's permission. According to the *New York Times* of February 19, 1956, Random House considered O'Neill's twenty-five-year restriction still valid and canceled its contract rather than publish. Yale University Press published the play and said in a subsequent letter to the *Times:*

American and Canadian publication rights in the play were given by Mr. O'Neill's widow, Carlotta Monterey O'Neill to the Yale University Library. . . . Having been assured that the playwright had lifted his original restriction concerning the publication of the play, the Library arranged for it publication. All royalties from the sale of the book under the terms of the deed of gift are to be paid to Yale University to set up an endowed Eugene O'Neill Memorial Fund. . . .

Long Day's Journey was performed in Stockholm even before the published play appeared on the American market. O'Neill had left it, evidently, as "a deathbed legacy to a nation which he felt had been more loyal to him than his own." (*Newsweek*, International Edition, February 20, 1956) Its reception was immediately enthusiastic. One Swedish critic, quoted in *Newsweek*, described the play as "one of the most powerful realistic dramas of the century. It's Ibsen's dramatic technique, but without his . . . symbolical overemphasis."

The critic hit home. *Long Day's Journey* is excruciatingly powerful because it is so painfully and consistently realistic. That is not intended to imply that literal realism is generally a criterion of dramatic power, but only that it frequently is in O'Neill's work, where realism is so often lost among unintegrated symbols, O'Neill's attempt at

poetry. In *Long Day's Journey* when the elder Tyrone
(James O'Neill, Sr.) tells his son Edmund (Eugene) that he
has the "makings of a poet," Edmund replies that he hasn't
even the makings. "I just stammered. That's the best I'll
ever do. . . . Well, it will be faithful realism at least.
Stammering is the native eloquence of us fog people." And
in *Long Day's Journey* the inarticulate child of fog speaks
with his native eloquence.

For all its realism the play is full of symbols. The fog
was O'Neill's first and last symbol of man's inability to
know himself, or other men, or his destiny. In Act I of
Long Day's Journey the sun is shining; in Act II the haze
gathers; in Act III a wall of fog stands thick against the
windowpanes. Through the fog at intervals a foghorn
moans, followed by a warning chorus of ship's bells—the
leitmotif of the family fate, sounding whenever that fate
asserts itself.

The interior set has its symbolic value too. The curtain
rises on "the living room of James Tyrone's summer house
in a morning in August, 1912. At rear are two double doorways with portieres. The one at the right leads into a
front parlor with the formally arranged, set appearance of
a room rarely occupied. The other opens on a dark, win-
dowless back parlor, never used except as a passageway
from living room to dining room." All the visible action
takes place before these doorways, in a shabby, cheaply
furnished living room lined with well-used books, the titles
of which are largely those of O'Neill's acknowledged influences. The family "lives" in that mid-region between the
bright formality of the exterior front parlor—the mask—
and the little-known dark of the rear room.

In that living room the four Tyrones torment them-

selves and each other, gradually stripping away every protective illusion until at the end each character must face
himself and the others without hope, but with a measure
of tolerance and pity. The focal point of the play is the
drug addiction of the mother and the family's early hope
that she has been cured. As this "pipe dream" vanishes, the
truths about the family emerge in anguished sequence.
Each confession elicits another confession, but in spite of
these often long and repetitious speeches the conflicts of
hate and love, guilt and accusation, lead to tense, exhaust-
ing, and brilliant drama. The driving force of the family
fate hurtles each of the characters into his own night and
causes him to take the others with him. All the Tyrones
are doomed to destroy and be destroyed, to be victimized
not only by each other but by the dead, for the dead have
willed them a heritage of disease, alcoholism, and drug
addiction, and have cursed them with the deeper ills of
alienation, conflict, and self-destructiveness.

This is O'Neill's own family, and their story was torn
from the depths of his consciousness. With an effort compounded of "tears and blood," O'Neill forced himself to
examine them honestly and objectively, from their own
points of view as well as his. The result was that the figures
most deeply rooted in that consciousness have emerged
from it not simply as symbols of their meaning to the
author, but as memorable, fully created individual personalities. But in each of these full portraits lurks the
outline of a psychological type who has appeared and
reappeared in O'Neill's work. Each type with its problems
dominated a period in O'Neill's development, but there
are only four Tyrones, and there are more than four stages
in O'Neill's own journey into night; the other stages are

to be found in the themes of this play and in O'Neill's very compulsion to write it.

Just as O'Neill's life journey began with his mother, his mature literary career began with "the searchers," those characters in his plays who were her direct descendants. Mary appears throughout the plays in two guises: what she was, and what her sons wanted her to be. She is the "eternal girl-woman," the wife and mother who longs to return (as in *Long Day's Journey* she does, in her drug fantasies) to the innocence of childhood and virginity. In *The Great God Brown* she was Dion's mother, whom he remembered as ". . . a sweet, strange girl, with affectionate, bewildered eyes as if God had locked her in a dark closet without any explanation. . . . I watched her die with the shy pride of one who has lengthened her dress and put up her hair. . . . The last time I looked, her purity had forgotten me, she was stainless and imperishable, and I knew my sobs were ugly and meaningless to her virginity. . . ."

Mary is also the inverse image of the Earth Mother for whom her sons long. Her hair was once the same "rare shade of reddish-brown," which symbolized prenatal freedom, security, and warmth in *Mourning Becomes Electra;* but Mary cannot give her sons this peace, and her hair is white. She is aware of her failure, and constantly apologizes for the whiteness and disorder of her hair. It represents not only age but guilt, for the graying began with her drug addiction, after the birth of Edmund. She knows that Edmund has inherited from her his extreme sensitivity, his "nervousness" and fear of life—and through her, from her father, his susceptiblity to tuberculosis. Edmund inherits from her also her sense of Fate, her awareness of

the fog, with her momentary attempts to see through it—
but alas, she has misplaced her glasses.

Mary's blindness is that of the protagonists of O'Neill's
earliest full-length plays, written in the years before 1919.
Like Mary, the searchers are aliens from self, seeking for
meaning and identity—but whenever they approach the
truth about themselves they must run away, back to the
fog, where, alone, they can "belong." Mary tells her son,
". . . I really love fog . . . it hides you from the world
and the world from you. . . . It's the foghorn that I hate.
It won't let you alone. It keeps reminding you, and warning you, and calling you back." (Act III, *Long Day's Journey Into Night*, p. 98) Edmund, too, the young O'Neill,
longs for that mysterious region where self was lost and
the tormenting masks of self can be lost again. He goes for
a walk in the fog because "The fog was where I wanted
to be. . . . Everything looked and sounded unreal. Nothing was what it is. . . . Who wants to see life as it is, if
they can help it? It's the three Gorgons in one. You look
in their faces and turn to stone. Or it's Pan. You see him
and you die. . . ." (Act IV, *Long Day's Journey Into
Night*, p. 131)

Mary describes the fate of all the searchers when she
says "None of us can help the things life has done to us.
They're done before you realize it, and once they're done
they make you do other things until at last everything
comes between you and what you'd like to be, and you've
lost your true self forever." (Act II, Sc. i, *Long Day's Journey Into Night*, p. 61) Ultimately, of course, this describes
the fate of most of O'Neill's characters, but it is most precisely and pointedly applicable to the protagonists of the
plays from *Beyond the Horizon* to *Anna Christie.* In the

fog of their past mistakes they grope for themselves as Mary does, and they see dimly the Gorgon and the Pan— the opposite masks of death and life—which they must face in order to survive. Like Mary, they vacillate between love and hate, a longing for companionship and a longing for privacy, for sexual fulfillment and for purity. Mary was a dreamer, and so were her son and all his searchers. They cling to their idealism and their hopeless hope, and they catch a glimpse of one vision which O'Neill never completely lost—the idea that the eternal seeker and idealist in man struggles to overcome the limitations of self, to make the "mystery behind things" express *him*. This is a tragic effort, doomed to failure, but it is all that can give value to the searchers' lives. For most of the searchers, however, the vision is only momentary; they remain, like Mary, lost and alienated somewhere between the self that limits and the self that aspires.

This bewildered, submissive mother was, of course, only one of the images by which O'Neill was haunted. The dominant image for the fanatics of the "extremist" plays (1919–21) is that of the ambitious, driving, and all but heartless father. The extremists find their way out of the fog by clinging to an aggressive, domineering image of the self. But this image turns out to be a false one, a mask which covers no face at all. The face, the real self, has been sold for the crazy power and illusive wealth represented by the mask. There can be no doubt, after reading *Long Day's Journey Into Night*, that regardless of what James O'Neill really was, to his son he represented this kind of pseudosolution to the search for self. He is the father of all O'Neill's proud, exploitive and grasping fathers—but self-deluded and pitiable, too, for Tyrone, in turn, was fashioned by *his* fathers, unable to escape the past which they created for him.

Tyrone, Sr., is the successful star actor of a romantic melodrama, as was the real James O'Neill. He has sacrificed wife and children to his need for secure wealth, denied him in his childhood. Obsessively, he invests his money in land, to the deprivation of his family. Here, of course, are Ephraim, Keeney, and Bartlett. With some justice his family blame Tyrone for most of their afflictions— his wife's need for drugs, one son's alcoholism and the other's illness and insecurity. Not only his desire for money, but his stubborn ignorance and defensive pride in his Irish-Catholic origin, re-enforcing his drive to outdo the Yankees, have been at the root of the family ills. The tragedy of Tyrone is that, like the other extremists, he has sold his soul for the illusion of success. He finally looks behind the mask when at the end of *Long Day's Journey* he confesses to Edmund:

Yes, maybe life overdid the lesson for me, and made a dollar worth too much. . . . I've never admitted this to anyone before, lad, but tonight I'm so heartsick I feel at the end of everything, and what's the use of fake pride and pretense. That God-damned play I bought for a song and made such a great success in—a great money success—it ruined me with its promise of an easy fortune. I didn't want to do anything else, and by the time I woke up to the fact I'd become a slave to the damned thing and did try other plays, it was too late. . . . What the hell was it I wanted to buy, I wonder, that was worth— Well, no matter. It's a late day for regrets. (Act III, *Long Day's Journey Into Night*, pp. 149–150)

Only the more sensitive of the extremists, like Tyrone, ever see the truth or realize that the real self has been lost. Indeed, among O'Neill's heroes, the sensitive ones alone are wholly alive, the sufferers and the creators. O'Neill took this positive view of sensitivity in the sequence of plays written between 1921 and 1927, when he believed most consciously and emphatically that the real order and justice of life lay in the tragic tension between opposites. His finders embrace this destiny and discover the answer to disunity in the unity of process, in the organic continuum in which opposition is the source of growth. In his own portrait of the artist as a young man in *Long Day's Journey,* O'Neill makes Edmund one of these tormented finders. In a long monologue addressed to his father, Edmund describes this stage of his development, when like his outcast namesake in *King Lear* he cries, "Thou nature, art my goddess!" If he cannot find a home with his family or with society, he can at least be absorbed into the processes of nature, especially those of the sea, where nature and the unconscious become symbolically one.

. . . I dissolved in the sea, became white sails and flying spray, became beauty and rhythm, became moonlight and the ship and the high dim-starred sky! I belonged, without past or future, within peace and unity and a wild joy, within something greater than my own life, or the life of Man, to Life itself! To God, if you want to put it that way. . . . Like a saint's vision of beatitude. Like the veil of things as they seem drawn back by an unseen hand. (Act III, *Long Day's Journey Into Night,* p. 153)

This was the vision of Juan, Kukachin, Jim, Abbie and Eben, Dion Brown, and finally, Lazarus. But

Then the hand lets the veil fall and you are alone, lost in the fog again, and you stumble on toward nowhere, for no good reason! . . . It was a great mistake, my being born a man, I would have been much more successful as a sea gull or a fish. As it is, I will always be a stranger who never feels at home, who does not really want and is not really wanted, who can never belong, who must always be a little in love with death! (Act III, *Long Day's Journey Into Night*, pp. 153–154)

Edmund is ill with tuberculosis—as O'Neill was in 1912 —and faces the possibility of death with a characteristic mixture of fear and longing. In addition, he learns with infuriated disgust that his father intends to economize on the cost of curing him by sending him to an inferior, state-supported sanitorium rather than to a private one. In the course of the play the father finally understands what he is doing and consents to send Edmund to a private hospital, where, indeed, O'Neill went. For all this apparent biographical accuracy of the portrait of the young O'Neill as Edmund, there is, as Dr. Weissman points out, at least one serious omission: O'Neill's marriage to Kathleen Jenkins in 1909 and his divorce from her in 1912, and the birth in 1910 of Eugene, Jr., whom O'Neill did not see until he was ten years old. O'Neill may have had any of several conscious reasons for suppressing this event in *Long Day's Journey*. Dr. Weissman suggests, however, that this omission amounted to an unconscious repression and rejection of the marriage itself, with all its overtones of O'Neill's inadequacy as a husband and father. Weissman explained the gap further in terms of O'Neill's identification with his mother:

O'Neill shows himself, denying his path of love, marriage and paternity, as his mother denies hers in her utterances. His drinking and wanderings serve to make him forget his commitments to earthly life, as his mother's addiction and somnambulance rendered her unaware of her husband and children. And now it seems that his tuberculosis for which he has to go to a sanitorium, as his mother goes to one for her addiction, will again remove them from their earthly life and attachments. (Philip Weissman, "Eugene O'Neill's Autobiographical Dramas," *Journal of the American Psychoanalytic Association*, V [July, 1957], p. 442)

In "dream, drunkenness, death," to use Engel's phrase, Edmund has succeeded in losing the self which tortured him with its ambivalence—toward itself and toward the conflicting father and mother images within it. In the "finders" period O'Neill saw, and demonstrated in his characters, the dualities which tore him apart. The only hope for integration lay, he knew, in his acceptance, if not reconciliation, of the dualities. But they could coexist only in the ecstatic visions of a transcendent oneness, visions which revealed themselves to be intellectualizations of real self-acceptance—theoretic, neurotic solutions to a neurotic struggle between the masks of the pride system. These may vanish for a while in the vision, but no real self is left to take their place—nothing but the mist, the fog, and through it the dismal horn of fate.

To this fate—the "true, fated reality" of *Mourning Becomes Electra*—O'Neill returned in his next group of plays, whose protagonists are called here "the trapped." The change in the plays was chiefly one of emphasis. The tension between opposites which the finders had considered a supporting framework of life now becomes a trap. The conflict of forces which the characters must attempt to reconcile or escape is that between the conscious mind and the unconscious—the modern equivalent of Fate. The protagonists' inevitable failure to control the unconscious mind ultimately makes them victims of destiny, not triumphant victors like their predecessors. Their struggle is no less heroic; in fact, it is more in the tradition of classic tragedy, and they approach more closely the dignity of the classic tragic hero than do the finders, for they *act* their "symbolical celebration of life," they do not see a vision of it or preach it.

Nina in *Strange Interlude* and Reuben in *Dynamo* spend their lives in an unwilled effort to escape the trap of self; so does Lavinia of *Mourning Becomes Electra*. The difference is that Lavinia almost does escape, until the death of Orin. Then she, too, is swallowed up by the family guilt; she turns on her heel and marches deliberately back into the self which alone can give her expiation. Her farewell words are, "I've got to punish myself. . . . It takes the Mannons to punish themselves for being born!"

And it took O'Neill to punish himself in writing *Long Day's Journey*. There he marches with Lavinia back to the only justice which can give him peace. His letter to his wife, published with the play, tells its own story. In it he thanks Mrs. O'Neill for the "love and tenderness which gave me the faith in love that enabled me to face my dead at last and write this play—write it with deep pity and understanding and forgiveness for ALL the four haunted Tyrones."

Long Day's Journey was penance, and in the penance

itself lay redemption. The penitent no longer cries for
another way out, for love and forgiveness through religious
faith, as he did in *Days Without End*. But the pattern of
that former yearning can still be traced in the posthumous
play. Just as in his early notes for *Days Without End*
O'Neill tried to avoid turning to Catholicism for the answer, so in *Long Day's Journey* the young Edmund rejects
his father's dogmatic and meaningless adherence to Catholicism, while at the same time Edmund sees his mother's
longing for faith, and feels that longing in himself. But as
O'Neill showed clearly in this family epitaph, formal religion could never be a telling force in his life, except as
it was identified with his mother; it offered no more reality
as a way out of the trap of self than did her way out by
morphine. The final curtain of *Long Day's Journey* falls
on the most pathetic and terrifying scene in the entire
canon. Mary has withdrawn into the dream world of a
past when, as a convent schoolgirl, she still had faith in
the Virgin.

. . . I knew she heard my prayer and would always love me
and see no harm ever came to me so long as I never lost my
faith in her. (*She pauses and a look of growing uneasiness
comes over her face. . . .*) That was in the winter of senior
year. Then in the spring something happened to me. Yes, I
remember. I fell in love with James Tyrone and was so happy
for a time. (*She stares before her in a sad dream. Tyrone stirs
in his chair. Edmund and Jamie remain motionless.*)

Tyrone stirs with the memory of old guilt which O'Neill
portrayed not only in *Long Day's Journey*, but in the person of Hickey in *The Iceman Cometh;* Edmund and James

are motionless, helpless with the paralysis of Larry in that play and of Jim Tyrone in *A Moon for the Misbegotten*. James, Sr.'s resemblance to Hickey emerges in Act III of *Long Day's Journey*, when Mary reveals that in the early years of their marriage Tyrone habitually disappeared, only to be brought home dead drunk to his young wife, waiting in "that ugly hotel room." At Mary's accusation, her son Edmund "bursts out with a look of accusing hate at his father," who, "overwhelmed by shame which he tries to hide," pleads, "Mary! Can't you forget—?" and Mary answers, like Hickey's wife, "No, dear. But I forgive. I always forgive you. So don't look so guilty." (Act III, *Long Day's Journey Into Night*, pp. 113–114)

Long Day's Journey is most closely related to the "fatal balance" plays in the character of James, Jr., whose story is continued in *A Moon for the Misbegotten*, set ten years later. Both the parents are dead, but the family Furies are still pursuing Jim to his death. He is cursed by all his parents' guilt, besides his own, all their conflicting love and hate, their drives toward escape and self-destruction. *Long Day's Journey* includes this theme but adds another —his relationship to Edmund.

Out of childhood jealousy, and envy of the promise shown in Edmund, Jamie deliberately sets his worshiping younger brother an example of cynicism and dissipated self-destruction, in the guise of sophistication and romantic adventure. Tyrone, Sr., constantly warns Edmund to beware of Jamie's "sneering serpent's tongue," and Jamie at last drunkenly confesses:

Mama and Papa are right. I've been rotten bad influence. . . . Did it on purpose to make a bum of you. Or part of me did. A big part. That part that's been dead so long. That hates life. My putting you wise so you'd learn from my mistakes. Believed that myself at times, but it's a fake. . . . Never wanted you succeed and make me look even worse by comparison. Wanted you to fail. Always jealous of you. Mama's boy, Papa's pet! . . . And it was your being born that started Mama on dope. I know that's not your fault, but all the same, God damn you, I can't help hating your guts! . . . But don't get wrong idea, Kid. I love you more than I hate you. . . . Make up your mind you've got to tie a can to me—get me out of your life—think of me as dead—tell people, "I had a brother, but he's dead." (Act III, *Long Day's Journey Into Night*, pp. 165–166)

But the influence was so deeply rooted that, dead or alive, O'Neill's brother became a part of him, identified often with himself. In the plays the figure of the elder brother changes. As Andy, in *Beyond the Horizon*, he is to be admired, then pitied for the mistakes which are his downfall. In *The Great God Brown*, he is to be feared as the trusted older friend, who steals up behind the child, Dion, when in Dion's words, "I was drawing a picture in the sand he couldn't draw, and hit me on the head with a stick and kicked out the picture in the sand. It wasn't what he'd done that made me cry, but him! I had loved and trusted him and suddenly the good God was disproved in his person. . . ." (Act II, Sc. iii, *Plays*, III, p. 295)

Jim's face with its "Mephistophelean cast," which sometimes, when he smiles without sneering, reveals a "humorous, romantic irresponsible Irish charm," is a constant shadow in O'Neill's consciousness. Often it is one of his own tormenting masks; the other, that of the poetic boy. Jim was born in O'Neill's first plays, and did not quite die in his last. His fate was foreshadowed as early as the curtain scene of *Beyond the Horizon,* when, as Andrew, he tried to fight the hopeless apathy into which Ruth had withdrawn. In the last three plays Ruth's night closes in upon Jim and upon O'Neill himself.

In *Iceman, Moon,* and *Long Day's Journey,* O'Neill returned to his tragic conception of life as an endless struggle between opposite images of the self. Now, however, the conflict is not only hopeless, as it was for "the trapped," but worthless. Man is not even endowed with dignity by virtue of his struggle; he is a bare, forked animal, unredeemed by heroism, who spends his life trying to live up to a lie, trying to perpetuate an illusory conception of himself. All values are equal; neither the self nor its conception has any real existence or importance, and all we can ask of each other is pity and forgiveness. So ends the lifelong day that dawned with O'Neill's searchers in the fog, children of his mother, Mary Tyrone, proceeded with the mad extremists led by his father, James, soared to ecstatic noon with the young Edmund and the finders—before the afternoon fog settled upon the trapped victims of the family fate. Hope in religion and family love briefly shone through, in *Days Without End* and *Ah, Wilderness,* only to fade back into the fog where nothing remains except, in the words of Archibald MacLeish,

> To feel how swift, how secretly,
> The shadow of the night comes on. . . .

Long Day's Journey Into Night is a tragedy with four heroes. It is tragedy—not melodrama or "slice of life"—because each of its protagonists is partly responsible for his own destruction and partly a victim of the family fate. This, I think, is the chief distinction between tragedy as a genre and other plays in which the protagonist suffers a change of fortune from good to bad. Tragedy is the superior art form, because it presents the human being's true dilemma. In melodrama the assumption is that man is totally responsible for his actions and that there is a simple eye-for-an-eye justice in the universe which rules that he will be punished if he is wicked and rewarded if he is virtuous. In the naturalistic drama the assumption is the opposite one—that man is the victim of forces utterly beyond his control—his glands, society, disease.

The truth, I think, is somewhere in between, and the last turn of the screw for the tragic hero is his discovery that he has been struck down not alone by villainy (his own or others) or fate, but by his own mistakes, rooted in his own character. And his mistakes could be ours, for he is "a man like ourselves."

This is not to say that any tragedy is necessarily a better play than any other serious drama. Some of O'Neill's plays which follow most closely the theoretical requirements of tragedy were his greatest failures as literature and drama, even when they were good theatrical spectacle. For this failure, there seem to be two principal reasons. First, O'Neill sometimes tries too hard to convince us of our "ennobling identity" with the characters on the stage; and second, he often *explains* the "symbolical celebration of life" instead of dramatizing it. Both these defects arise from O'Neill's own tragic flaw, his neurosis.

The inert, paralyzed state of mind of the characters in the last three plays—a condition from which death alone can bring release—is one logical conclusion to be drawn from the philosophy that life is suspended between hopelessly divergent opposites. But the entire process of formulating such a theory springs not from logic, but from the necessity of a sick mind to fulfill its own needs. O'Neill called this drive the "sickness of today," and so it is. But then, it was the sickness also of the medieval monk, wrestling with his "dryness of spirit." Psychology and sociology have made us more aware today than ever before of the quiet desperation in which most men lead their lives, in an "other-directed" society where all goals are impositions from without. The tragic situation of modern man lies in the abdication of the real individual self from the position of authority and decision-making in favor of self-images drawn from society's expectations. O'Neill struck the right note for twentieth-century tragedy; Arthur Miller and Tennessee Williams have developed his theme.

Nevertheless, the crippling extreme to which the ailment is portrayed in O'Neill's plays is, fortunately, rare and more curable than he thought. Most sensitive people at one time or another have felt its symptoms. They have been there; but they have come back. Men manage somehow to go about their business, symbolizing in action—humdrum and prosaic though it may be—their unconscious affirmation of the tragic fate, their quiet acceptance of the fact that evil is the necessary concomitant of good. O'Neill has conceptualized for us our unconscious conflicts, our faith and despair, and when his plays fail it is not because of banality of subject matter, but because of his mistaken conviction that, as Lazarus puts it, "Life is for each man a solitary cell whose walls are mirrors." No—not for each man, nor even for most men, but only for O'Neill and those sick, tragic heroes whose egotism has so surrounded them with self-images that they are doomed to a lifelong search for reality amid illusions, or to self-destruction—their own fall through pride.

O'Neill is at his best when he acknowledges the personal, esoteric nature of the struggle and leaves the audience to make the application to itself. But his urge to shout the universality of a struggle whose very essence is its inwardness is related to his justified suspicion of "happy endings." The only logical happy ending to an inner conflict is its cessation or a deeply felt insight into it which makes it worthwhile or meaningful to the protagonist. When the conflict ceases simply because all passion is spent, as in *Strange Interlude,* or because the hero has given up the fight altogether and sought relief in death, as in *The Iceman Cometh* and *A Moon for the Misbegotten,* the ending is unspectacular but logical. If the audience accepts the premises of the play, it accepts the conclusion.

But in his eagerness to make some of his dramas tragic, rather than merely "pessimistic," O'Neill has attempted to explain the inexplicable, to bring home to the audience the meaning of tragic affirmation—a mysterious term whose real significance is implied in the moral order and in the heroism of the action. The plays with weakest conclusions end in paeans of praise for tragic struggle, and the paean usually expresses a mystical insight. It is, in a sense, just what O'Neill was trying to avoid, a kind of happy ending, an explanation to the audience of the positive value of the struggle, which the audience should feel in the action itself. O'Neill's greatest tragedies are those in which the protagonist is brought to his knees by fate, unredeemed by any revelation except that recognition of his own responsibility which follows as a logical consequence of the action. His best explanation of the meaning of dramatic tragedy is perhaps the final comment of Smithers in *The Emperor Jones,* "Gawd blimey, but yer died in the 'eighth o'style, any'ow!'"

The pace of the action and the ratio of exposition to drama in O'Neill's plays are partly a problem in the mechanics of play-making, but are more directly correlated to the inwardness of the action, and therefore to the psychological state of the author. A play can be equally dramatic whether its action is that of outward conflict or that of inner conflict, taking place within the "theater of the soul." Even an inner conflict can be dramatized in outward activity; or it can be projected in expressionistic symbols from the mind of the protagonist, or it can be described in dialogue. All these methods, of course, are combined in the work of most modern dramatists. The danger of emphasis on the last method is that the play may become a long series of speeches and counter-speeches: self-analysis—reaction of the listener—then *his* self-analysis, and so on *ad taedium.* When the action is entirely inward and is portrayed in this manner, then the burden of creating suspense and interest is upon the director and the actors, who must work like fiends to overcome the prolixity of the script.

The dramatic conflict of *The Emperor Jones* and *The Hairy Ape* takes place chiefly within the mind of the protagonist, although the conflict begins and ends as a war with outer reality. In these plays, the inner struggle is projected in vital, fast-moving symbolic action and in vivid expressionistic symbols. In *Mourning Becomes Electra* and *Strange Interlude,* while the characters are still in contact with the outside world, they tell us about the inner world in the long soliloquies which slow the dramatic movement of these and all the subsequent plays. The recently discovered cycle play, *More Stately Mansions,* is said to take ten hours in performance. It is safe to speculate that most of that time is spent in long self-analyses, and that O'Neill was probably right when he withheld the play from production in its present form.

The progress of O'Neill's mind was steadily away from an outer world where purposeful activity and event, or "plot," were important, through an inner world where conflict is important, to an innermost world where nothing is important. Underlying the soliloquies in *Strange Interlude* and *Mourning Becomes Electra,* there is still a plot; the characters must act and must participate in life. But in *The Iceman Cometh* the crux of the play is the *inability* of the characters to act. Although here the use of the long soliloquy is perfectly consistent with the characterizations, O'Neill is forced for dramatic suspense to resort to the device of the delayed and long-awaited arrival of a principal character throughout the first half of the play. In *Long Day's Journey* all significant action has taken place in the past; the present consequence is despair. In *A Moon for the Misbegotten* O'Neill relinquishes all considerations of outer action; he depends for plot on mechanical clichés, and for character development on exposition. The world of outer action becomes a structure of cardboard and canvas, the world of the inner life, a desert of nothing, where even the vision of death as an oasis is a mirage.

Eugene O'Neill died on November 27, 1953. The strange, dark interlude that had been his life was finally ended, and the hated self was now, at last, annihilated.

As if he wished to obliterate even the memory of that self, O'Neill, according to newspaper accounts of his death (*Boston Post,* December 3, 1953), gave specific orders that there should be no ceremony at his burial, no mourners except his wife, doctor, and nurse, no embellishments on the casket, and no inscription on the stone except the one word, "O'Neill." Although the actual inscription is a conventional one, the request for that epitaph bears ironic witness to the unconscious egotism and the self-effacement which had torn his life between them.

The whole world knows now of O'Neill's affliction by Parkinson's disease in the last decade of his life. The tremor of his hands which had for years made writing difficult for him (he wrote all his early drafts of plays in longhand) now became an uncontrollable jerking palsy, and writing was impossible. When physical death finally came, it was for O'Neill just another stage in the life cycle, welcome and somewhat belated. The only life he valued, that of the productive dramatist, had long since ended, and all his final work had been "by way of obit." He chronicled the life and death of the artist in his plays; future biography, now in progress, will fill in the factual details. It will explain precise relationships between O'Neill's "nervous breakdowns," his physical ailments—including tuberculosis and the slow onslaught of Parkinson's disease—and the philosophy of the plays. It will clarify the connections between the heroes of the plays and the behavior of their author—his strange combination of cruelty and compassion toward himself and others.

Whatever the verdict of posterity, there was something Promethean about this man who strove with defiant integrity to project through the drama his own vision of the truth. The scope of that vision—breadth and limitation, clarity and distortion—sprang from the inward agony of a mind doomed endlessly to feed upon itself. Inevitably, that very torment which had given birth to the vision finally destroyed it.

In the last plays O'Neill walked in the valley not of death alone, but of nothingness in which all values are illusions and all meaning fades before the terror of ambiguity. Like Poe, Melville, and Dostoevsky, O'Neill was driven to dedicate a lifetime of work to the celebration of the dreadful journey. His heroes, like theirs, are doomed to assert their humanity by a struggle with ghosts in the dark night of the soul. The opponent is that most vicious and evasive of all enemies, the self. By him alone can the hero be vanquished, and this is at once his destruction and his triumph, his fall and his resurrection. In the magnificent futility of the struggle is a fragment, at least, of the history of humanity.

POSTSCRIPT

Since the first printing of this book, O'Neill's one-act play, *Hughie* (see page 157) has been published (Yale University Press, 1959), and previous to publication was performed in Sweden in Stockholm's Royal Dramatic Theater. (For an account of this performance, see Henry Hewes, "Broadway Postscript," *Saturday Review*, October 4, 1958.) This fascinating forty-minute play comes from the "Fatal Balance" period. Its theme is that of *The Iceman Cometh* and *A Touch of the Poet;* the life-attitude expressed in it is that of *Long Day's Journey Into Night*. The protagonist is a small-time gambler, down on his luck, who in O'Neill's words is "consciously a Broadway sport and a Wise Guy." (*Hughie*, p. 9) The only person who had ever accepted and reinforced this illusory self-image of the gambler was Hughie, the night clerk at the run-down hotel where the gambler lives. But Hughie has just died; the gambler has just returned from several days of drunkenness following the funeral, to find a new night clerk in Hughie's place. With a mixture of bravado and pathos, the gambler tells the clerk of his relationship with Hughie. To the gambler Hughie had been a lovable sucker who admired him and whom he, in turn, protected. At first the new night clerk pays no attention to the guest's long monologue, but gradually his own despair and frustration convince him that the speaker *is* the sport he thinks he is. The new clerk takes the place of the old one in his naive respect for the gambler as the representative of an adventurous, sophisticated world to which the clerk, himself, would like to belong but never can. Thus the "pipe dreams" of the gambler are revived by those of the clerk.

As in all the last plays, the action takes place in "hope's back room," at the end of a long journey into night. The play is performed against a backdrop of death, despair, and darkness. It is no accident that the clerk is the *night* clerk, or that his name (Hughes) and age are the same as the dead Hughie's. His face is expressionless and cadaverous; he says very little, but his thoughts, detailed in the stage directions, are all of night and death. The establishment of contact between the two men and the restoration of illusion provide a kind of hope for them both, but it is a pathetically "hopeless hope." The gambler's life story is told in retrospect; his self-image is the ghost of a dead past, and it alone stands between him and death. When he rolls the dice with the clerk at the final curtain he is gambling with death, and we are reminded that *Hughie* was intended to be the first play in the cycle called *By Way of Obit*.

This one-act play contains some of O'Neill's most powerful and sensitive writing. It is less a play to be acted in the theater than a character sketch in the form of soliloquy and unspoken asides. The clerk is portrayed almost entirely by stage directions in which he listens to the sounds of the night and to his own thoughts rather than to the words of the gambler. All the action is inward, expressed in expository speeches and stage directions. Still, this is a beautiful, moving, and valuable addition to O'Neill's work; its very defects are only further evidence of the static, paralyzed view of life revealed in the last plays.

Doris Falk

April, 1959

NOTES

THEME

1 Edwin A. Engel, *The Haunted Heroes of Eugene O'Neill* (Cambridge, Mass., 1953).

QUESTION

1 *The American Spectator Yearbook* (New York, 1934), pp. 166–167.
2 *Thirst and Other One-Act Plays* (Boston, 1914). The other titles are *The Web, Warnings,* and *Recklessness.*
3 *The Plays of Eugene O'Neill,* 3 vols. (New York, 1954), I, pp. 477–490. This will hereafter be cited as *Plays.* Page references for all the plays up to and including *The Iceman Cometh* are to this edition.
4 Richard Dana Skinner, *Eugene O'Neill, A Poet's Quest* (New York, 1935), p. viii.
5 Cf. Henry Alonzo Myers, "The Meaning of *Moby Dick,*" in *Tragedy: A View of Life* (Ithaca, N.Y., 1956), p. 72.

THE SEARCHERS

1 Arthur Hobson Quinn, *A History of the American Drama from the Civil War to the Present Day,* 2 vols. (New York, 1945), II, p. 199.
2 The manuscript is to be found in the Yale University Library.
3 *The Plays of Eugene O'Neill,* Wilderness Edition, 12 vols. (New York, 1934), V, p. xi.
4 Erich Fromm, *Man for Himself* (New York, 1947), p. 40. The title of the section of Fromm's book in which this passage occurs is "The Existential and Historical Dichotomies in Man." His ideas resemble so closely some of the theses of Sartrian existentialism that Fromm felt called upon to declare his independence of Sartre—at the time of writing, he had not yet had "access to Sartre's main philosophical opus." (p. 41)
5 Mary B. Mullett, "The Extraordinary Story of Eugene O'Neill," *American Magazine,* XCIV (November, 1922), p. 118.
6 Barrett Clark, *Eugene O'Neill: The Man and His Plays* (New York, 1948), p. 68.
7 Isaac Goldberg, *The Theatre of George Jean Nathan* (New York, 1926), p. 154.
8 Carl Gustav Jung, *The Integration of the Personality,* trans. Stanley M. Dell (New York, 1939), p. 103.

THE EXTREMISTS

1 Letter to Barrett Clark concerning *Mourning Becomes Electra*, quoted in Clark's *Eugene O'Neill: The Man and His Plays* (New York, 1948), p. 136.
2 Carl Gustav Jung, "Psychology and Literature," in *Modern Man in Search of a Soul*, trans. W. S. Dell and C. F. Baynes (New York, 1923), p. 199.

THE FINDERS

1 Carl Gustav Jung, *The Integration of the Personality*, trans. by Stanley M. Dell (New York, 1939), p. 20.
2 *Ibid.*, pp. 91–92.
3 Carl Gustav Jung, quoted in Jolan Jacobi, *The Psychology of Jung* (New Haven, 1943), p. 19.
4 Mary B. Mullett, "The Extraordinary Story of Eugene O'Neill," *American Magazine* (November, 1922), p. 118.
5 Carl Gustav Jung, *Two Essays in Analytical Psychology* (London and New York, 1928), p. 183.
6 Karen Horney, *Neurosis and Human Growth* (New York, 1950), p. 17.
7 Francis Ferguson, "Eugene O'Neill," in *Literary Opinion in America*, ed. by Morton Dauwen Zabel (New York, 1937), p. 322.
8 Eugene O'Neill, "Memoranda on Masks," *American Spectator Yearbook* (New York, 1934), p. 161.

THE TRAPPED

1 Barrett Clark, *Eugene O'Neill: The Man and His Plays* (New York, 1948), p. 111. Sophus Keith Winther, *Eugene O'Neill, A Critical Study* (New York, 1934), p. 51.
2 Richard Dana Skinner, *Eugene O'Neill, A Poet's Quest* (New York, 1935).
3 *The American Mercury*, XVI (January, 1929), p. 119.
4 Eugene O'Neill, "Working Notes and Extracts from a Fragmentary Work Diary," in *Chief European Theories of the Drama, American Supplement*, ed. by Barrett H. Clark (New York, 1947), p. 533.
5 *Ibid.*, p. 535.
6 *Ibid.*, p. 533.
7 *Ibid.*, p. 534.
8 "Aristotle's Poetics," *Aristotle's Theory of Poetry and Fine Arts*, trans. by S. H. Butcher (New York, 1951), p. 27.
9 *Ibid.*, p. 29.

10 The passage referred to reads in part as follows:

> . . . the change of fortune presented must not be the spectacle of a virtuous man brought from prosperity to adversity: for this moves neither pity nor fear; it merely shocks us. Nor, again, that of a bad man passing from adversity to prosperity. . . . Nor again, should the downfall of the utter villain be exhibited. A plot of this kind would, doubtless, satisfy the moral sense, but it would inspire neither pity nor fear; for pity is aroused by unmerited misfortune, fear by the misfortune of a man like ourselves. . . . a man who is not eminently good and just, yet whose misfortune is brought about not by vice or depravity, but by some error or frailty.

11 Henry Alonzo Myers, *Tragedy, a View of Life* (Ithaca, N.Y., 1956), pp. 11–12.

THE WAY OUT

1 *The Plays of Eugene O'Neill,* Wilderness Edition, 12 vols. (New York, 1934) III, pp. xi, xii.
2 Eugene O'Neill, "Memoranda on Masks," *American Spectator Year-book* (New York, 1934), p. 162.
3 These are in the Yale University Library.
4 Part III, Act IV, Sc. iii, August Strindberg, *To Damascus,* trans. by Sam E. Davidson, *Poet Lore,* XLII (1933–35), p. 264. (The quotation is complete, the punctuation that of the translation; the dots are not ellipses.)

FATAL BALANCE

1 *A Tale of Possessors Self-Dispossessed* was intended to relate the history of an Irish family in America. In a letter to Barrett Clark, O'Neill said, "There will be nothing of *Ah, Wilderness!* or *Days Without End* in this Cycle. They were an interlude. The Cycle goes back to my old vein of ironic tragedy—with, I hope, added psychological depth and insight." Barrett Clark, *Eugene O'Neill: The Man and His Plays* (New York, 1948), p. 144.

The following plan was furnished by Dr. Donald C. Gallup, curator of the Collection of American Literature (including, of course, the Eugene O'Neill Collection) at the Yale University Library:

A Tale of Possessors Self-Dispossessed: A Cycle of Eleven Plays
I–II. The Greed of the Meek [Play as written covering 1776–93

was to be expanded into two plays, one 1755–57, the
other 1775]

III–IV. And Give Me Death [Play as written covering 1806–07
was to be expanded into two plays, one 1783–94, the
other 1804–05]

V.	A Touch of the Poet	1828
VI.	More Stately Mansions	1837–42['46?]
VII.	The Calms of Capricorn	1857
VIII.	The Earth's the Limit	1858–60
IX.	Nothing is Lost Save Honor	1862–70
X.	The Man on Iron Horseback	1876–93
XI.	[The Hair of the Dog]	1900–32

The completed plays were written in this order:

A Touch of the Poet
And Give Me Death (1st draft)
The Greed of the Meek (1st draft)
More Stately Mansions (1st draft)

Dr. Gallup adds the following information: " 'A Touch of the
Poet' was at one time O'Neill's title for the entire cycle and 'The
Hair of the Dog' was then the title for the play which later became
'A Touch of the Poet.' I gather from O'Neill's notes that he had de-
cided to use 'The Hair of the Dog' as title for the final play. In
various lists of the cycle plays in his hand, the final play is untitled."

2 Clark, *Eugene O'Neill: The Man and His Plays*, p. 154.
3 *Ibid.*, p. 147.
4 *Ibid.*, p. 145.
5 George Jean Nathan, *The Intimate Notebooks of George Jean Nathan*
(New York, 1932), p. 33.
6 *The New York Times*, November 4, 1956.

INDEX

Abbie, 76, 96–99, 187
Ah, Wilderness! 145, 194
Ahab, parallels with, 22, 60, 65
Alexander, Doris, 136, 142
All God's Chillun Got Wings (1923), 87–90
Allegory of masks, 99–108
And Give Me Death (1934–1943), 156–157
Andrew, 37–43, 193
Anna Christie (Chris Christopherson) (1919, 1920), 27–28, 45, 48–52
Aristotle, 5, 136–143, 163
  on tragedy, 136–143

Bartlett, 62–65, 77, 186
Beatriz, 76, 81–83
Beyond the Horizon (1917, 1919), 19, 27–28, 37–45, 47, 51, 58, 60, 193, 194
Bound East for Cardiff (1914), 15, 20–22, 24, 43, 45, 164
Brant, Adam, 130–134
Brown, Billy, 99–108
"businessman, the," symbol of, 19
By Way of Obit (1934–1943), 156–157

Catholicism, 146–155, 173, 191
Chris, 28, 48–52, 53, 57, 78

Christine, 131–133
church, the, 26, 147–155
Clark, Barrett, 66, 148, 164
Con, 165–170
conflict, of opposites, 4–5, 24, 25–
    28, 42–43, 92–94, 97–99, 194
    between sexes, 77, 87, 88–90
    within self, 84–85, 157–164
Curtis, 72–76, 77–78
Cybel, 76, 86, 101, 105, 108, 121–
    122, 127–128

Days Without End (1931–1934),
    18, 79, 114, 145–155, 194
death, concept of, 20–21, 109–111,
    144, 157–159, 162–165
    and life, conflict of, 129–143,
    153–154
Desire Under the Elms (1924), 93–
    99, 177
Diff'rent (1920), 61, 71–72
Dion, 99–108, 117, 175, 187
Dionysus, theme of, 100–101, 106,
    108, 113–114
Dynamo (1928), 19, 121, 126–129,
    148

Earth Mother, symbol of, 76, 86,
    101–105, 108, 121–122, 127–
    128, 164, 169, 177, 183–184
Eben, 94–98, 117, 187
Edmund, 181–189, 191–193
Eileen, 45–48
Eleanor, 85–87
Electra complex, 94, 129–143
Ella, 87–90
Elsa, 148–150
Emma, 71–72
Emperor Jones, The (1920), 52, 61,
    66–71, 198
Engel, Edwin, 9, 189
Ephraim, 94–99, 117, 186
"epiphany," or self-recognition, 43–
    44, 90, 138

ethos, of O'Neill characters, 139–
    143, 163
existentialism, parallels in O'Neill
    to, 34–35, 87, 163
"extremists, the," driven to madness
    or death, 60, 61–78

"Fall through Pride," 4–13, 139–
    143
family fate, 145–146, 165, 171,
    181–188
"fatal balance," between masks of
    self, 156–178, 192–194
father, symbol of, 93–94, 121–143,
    167, 185–186
father-mother, as conflicting oppo-
    sites, 93–94
Faust-Mephistopheles conflict, 147–
    155, 175
Fergusson, Francis, 118–119
Fife, Mrs., 76, 127–128
"finders," the, and conflict of mys-
    ticism and materialism, 79–
    120, 187–189
First Man, The (1921), 61, 72–75
Fog (1913–1914), 19
Fountain, The (1921–1927), 79–84
Frazer, Mr., 15–19
Frazer, Mrs., 15–19, 23, 57, 60
freedom and self-fulfillment, theme
    of, 85–86
Freud, Sigmund, influence of, 6, 7,
    66, 136
Fromm, Erich, philosophy of, 7–9,
    36–37, 163

girl-woman, eternal, 100, 183
God, concept of, 95–99, 100–108,
    125–128
Gold (1920), 61, 62–65
Great God Brown, The (1925), 19,
    26, 99–108, 117, 193
Greed of the Meek, The (1934–
    1943), 156–157

Hairy Ape, The (1917, 1921), 10, 27–35, 36, 52, 55, 57, 58, 98, 198
Hamlet, 27
Harry, 158–160, 162
Hickey, 159–162, 191–192
Horney, Karen, psychoanalytic theories of, parallels in O'Neill to, 7-9, 53–60, 71, 77, 88, 97, 115–119, 147, 162
hubris, 5, 139–142

Ibsen, Henrik, works of, parallels in O'Neill to, 77
Iceman Cometh, The (1939), 15, 28, 94, 156–166, 194, 197, 199
identity, search for, 53–60
Ile (1917), 15, 22–24

Jamie, 171–177, 191–194
Jim, 87–90, 117, 187
Jimmy the Priest's, New York, 28–29, 164–165
John, 146–153, 175
Jones, Brutus, 66–70, 77
Josie, 173–177
Jung, Carl G., psychoanalytic theories of, parallels in O'Neill to, 6–8, 51–52, 65–66, 70, 76–77, 84, 107–108, 110, 136, 162
animus and *anima,* 76
ideas and symbols of, in *Great God Brown,* 107–108

Keeney, Captain, 22–24, 57, 60, 62, 186
Keeney, Mrs., 22–24
Kierkegaard, S. A., philosophy of, parallels in O'Neill to, 24, 35, 54, 162
King Lear, 27
Kublai Kaan, **90–93**
Kukachin, 76, 90–93, 117, 187

Lao-tse, philosophy of, parallels in O'Neill to, 5, 84
Larry, 60, 159–164
Lavinia, 130–135, 190
Lazarus, 117, 187
Lazarus Laughed (1925–1927), 108–114
Leeds, Professor, 122–124
Long Day's Journey Into Night (1940–1941), 15, 19–20, 149, 165, 170–171, 179–195, 198
Lost Plays of Eugene O'Neill, The (1950, 1958), 15
love, conflict in, 87, 88–90

man, as artist or creative spirit, 19, 48, 86, 99–108
Marco Millions (1923–1925), 19, 90–93
Marco Polo, 90–93, 117
Margaret, 76, 99–108, 117
Martha, 73–76
Mary, 176–178, 183–186
Masks, Memoranda on, 147
masks, symbolism of, 14–15, 18–20, 24, 33–34, 62, 64 77–78, 85, 96, 98, 99–108, 116–118, 121, 126–128, 130–132, 145–148, 157, 173, 175–176, 185–187, 189
use of, 99–108
Michael, 85–87
Mildred, 30–31
modern society, conflicting elements of, O'Neill's allegory, 100–108, 128
Moon for the Misbegotten, A (1943), 15, 94, 156–157, 171–177, 197, 199
More Stately Mansions (1934–1943), 156–157, 199
mother, symbol of, 93–94, 121–122, 125–126, 127–128, 136, 151, 161, 167, 174–178, 183–185

Mourning Becomes Electra (1931), 98, 121, 177, 189–190, 198, 199
mysticism and materialism, 90–93, 94–99

Nathan, George Jean, O'Neill's letters to, 48–49, 128, 148
natural process, theme of, 4–5, 109–114
"need to belong," 36–37
Neo-Freudian theory, parallels in O'Neill to, 7–9, 36–37
neurotic pride, 140–143
Nietzsche, Friedrich, writings of, parallels in O'Neill to, 5, 8, 44, 84, 108, 117–118
Nina, 122–126, 142, 190
Nora, 166–170

Oedipus complex, 94, 107–108, 129
O'Neill, Eugene, quoted, 20, 25–26, 28–29, 34, 36, 37–38, 48–49, 51, 100–101, 104–105, 129, 130, 145, 150, 164
Orestes, story of, parallels in O'Neill to, 27, 95n., 129–136
Orin, 130–134

Paddy, 28–29, 30
paganism, and Christianity, conflict of, 100–108
Phil, 173–175
Ponce de León, 79–84, 117, 187
pride, 4–5, 7–8, 99
and love, conflict of, 129–143
pride system, struggle of "finders" in, 117–119, 189
prideful illusion, and shameful reality, conflict of, 157–162, 165–170
pseudosolution, in Horney's theory, 59–60, 64, 185
psychoanalysis, relation to plays, 5–13, 27, 35–37

psychoanalytic symbols, use of, 5–13
Puritanism, and freedom, conflict of, 129–143

Quinn, Arthur Hobson, O'Neill's letter to (1925), 25–26

religion, *see* church
Research in Marriage, A, as source, 136
Reuben, 126–129, 190
Robert, 37–43, 52, 53, 58, 60, 78
Roylston, 15–19, 23
Ruth, 37–43, 60

Sara, 166–170
Schopenhauer, Arthur, 84, 110n., 142
"searchers for self," the, theme of, 25–60, 183–185
self, concept of, 24, 25–28
search for, 42–45, 90, 111–120, 138–143, 162
self-hatred, pattern of, in the plays, 117–118, 174–177
self-images, 158, 162, 168–169, 194, 196
Servitude (ca. 1914), 15–19, 24, 45, 48, 60
Sievers, W. D., 136
Skinner, Richard Dana, 10, 122
soliloquy, device of, 126
Stephen, 45–48, 52, 53, 58, 60, 78
Strange Interlude (1927), 110, 121–126, 197, 198, 199
Straw, The (1917, 1919), 27–28, 45–48, 51, 58, 97
parallel in O'Neill's life, 47–48
Strindberg, August, writings of, parallels in O'Neill to, 77, 84, 87, 153–154
subconscious, the, as force in man's character, 25–27

suicide, O'Neill's attitude toward, 162–163, 165
symbolic setting, use of, 19–20, 181
symbols, 26, 70, 86–87, 98–99, 100–108, 126, 127–128, 129–135

Tale of Possessors Self-Dispossessed, A (1934–1943), 156–157
Touch of the Poet, A (1943–1957), 28, 156–157, 165–170
tragedy, *see* Aristotle
tragic drama, O'Neill's philosophy of, 112–114, 194–199
"trapped," the, conflict between conscious mind and unconscious, 121–143, 189–194

Tyrone, Sr., 181–182, 185–187, 191
"way out, the," escape from duality, 144–155
Weissman, Dr. Philip, "Eugene O'Neill's Autobiographical Dramas," 9, 188–189
Welded (1922–1924), 85–87, 117, 148
woman, O'Neill's conception of, 125
"Working Notes and Extracts from a Fragmentary Work Diary," 129, 130, 131

Yank (*Bound East for Cardiff*), 20–22
Yank (*The Hairy Ape*), 29–36, 52, 53, 55, 57, 58, 60